# THE BEAR'S HUG

## Christian Belief
## and the Soviet State

*1917-1986*

Gerald Buss

WILLIAM B. EERDMANS PUBLISHING COMPANY
GRAND RAPIDS, MICHIGAN

Copyright © 1987 By Gerald Buss

First published 1987 in Great Britain
by Hodder and Stoughton Ltd., London

This edition published 1987 through special arrangement with
Hodder and Stoughton
by Wm. B. Eerdmans Publishing Co., 255 Jefferson Ave. SE,
Grand Rapids, Mich. 49503

**Library of Congress Cataloging-in-Publication Data**

Buss, Gerald, 1936-
   The bear's hug.

   Bibliography: p. 215
   Includes index.
   1. Russkai pravoslavnaia tserkov — History — 20th century.
   2. Orthodox Eastern Church — Soviet Union — History — 20th century.
   3. Church and state — Soviet Union — History — 20th century.
   4. Persecution — Soviet Union — History — 20th century.
   5. Soviet Union — Church history — 1917-    .  II. Title.
   BX492.B87   1987     323.44'2'0947     87-19639

ISBN 0-8028-0324-5

# Contents

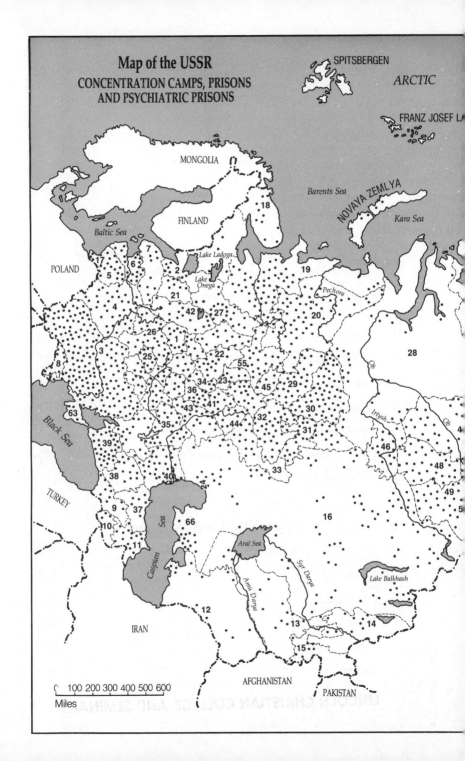

# Map of the USSR
## CONCENTRATION CAMPS, PRISONS AND PSYCHIATRIC PRISONS

SPITSBERGEN

ARCTIC

FRANZ JOSEF LA

MONGOLIA

FINLAND

Barents Sea

NOVAYA ZEMLYA

Kara Sea

Baltic Sea

POLAND

Lake Ladoga

Lake Onega

Pechora

Black Sea

TURKEY

Ob

Irtysh

Ob

Aral Sea

Syr Darya

Amu Darya

Lake Balkhash

Caspian Sea

IRAN

AFGHANISTAN

PAKISTAN

0  100 200 300 400 500 600
Miles

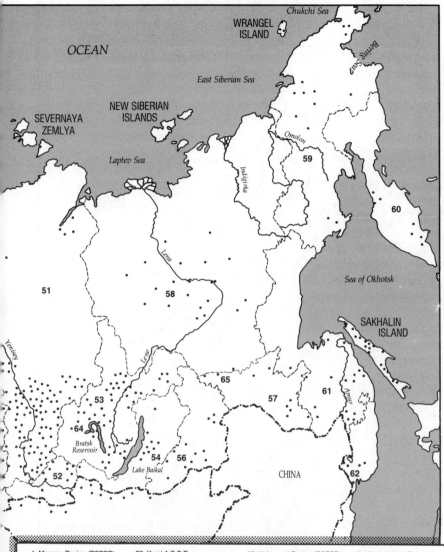

OCEAN

*Chukchi Sea*

WRANGEL ISLAND

*East Siberian Sea*

*Bering Sea*

NEW SIBERIAN ISLANDS

SEVERNAYA ZEMLYA

*Omolon*

59

*Laptev Sea*

*Indigirka*

60

*Lena*

*Sea of Okhotsk*

51

58

SAKHALIN ISLAND

*Yenisey*

*Lena*

53

65

57

61

*Amur*

64

*Bratsk Reservoir*

54    56

52

*Lake Baikal*

CHINA

62

1. Moscow Region (RSFSR)
2. Leningrad Region (RSFSR)
3. Ukrainian S.S.R.
4. Belorussian S.S.R.
5. Lithuanian S.S.R.
6. Latvian S.S.R.
7. Estonian S.S.R.
8. Moldavian S.S.R.
9. Georgian S.S.R.
10. Armenian S.S.R.
11. Azerbaidzhan S.S.R.
12. Turkmen S.S.R.
13. Uzbek S.S.R.
14. Kirghiz S.S.R.
15. Tadzhik S.S.R.
16. Kazakh S.S.R.
17. Kaliningrad Region (RSFSR)
18. Murmansk Region (RSFSR)
19. Arkhangel'sk Region (RSFSR)

20. Komi A.S.S.R.
21. Novgorod Region (RSFSR)
22. Gor'kii Region (RSFSR)
23. Tatar A.S.S.R.
24. Petrozavodsk Region
25. Orel, Kursk, Tula, Kaluga, Lipetsk Regions (RSFSR)
26. Pskov, Vladimir, Bryansk, Kalinin, Smolensk Regions (RSFSR)
27. Vologda, Kostroma, Kirov, Izhevsk Regions (RSFSR)
28. Tvumen Region (RSFSR)
29. Perm Region (RSFSR)
30. Sverdlovsk Region (RSFSR)
31. Chelyabinsk Region (RSFSR)
32. Bashkir A.S.S.R.
33. Orenburg Region (RSFSR)
34. Mordovian A.S.S.R.

35. Volgograd Region (RSFSR)
36. Penza Region (RSFSR)
37. Kalmyk and Daghestan A.S.S.R.
38. Stavropol' Territory
39. Krasnodar Territory and Rostov Region
40. Astrakhan' Region (RSFSR)
41. Ul'yanovsk Region (RSFSR)
42. Yaroslavl' Region (RSFSR)
43. Saratov Region (RSFSR)
44. Kuibyshev Region (RSFSR)
45. Udmurt A.S.S.R.
46. Omsk Region (RSFSR)
47. Tomsk Region (RSFSR)
48. Novosibirsk Region (RSFSR)
49. Altai Territory
50. Gorno-Altai Autonomous Region (RSFSR)

51. Krasnoyarsk Territory
52. Tuva A.S.S.R.
53. Irkutsk Region
54. Buryat A.S.S.R.
55. Chuvash A.S.S.R.
56. Chita Region
57. Amur Region
58. Yakutsk A.S.S.R.
59. Magadan Region
60. Kamchatka Region
61. Khabarovsk Territory
62. Primorsk Territory
63. Crimean Region
64. Taishet ,,Ozerlag''
65. BAM
66. Mangyshlak Peninsula

**THE SOVIET UNION IN
THE SECOND WORLD WAR**

FINLAND

USSR

Leningrad

ESTONIA

Pskov

Riga
LATVIA

Moscow

LITHUANIA

EAST
PRUSSIA

Smolensk

Brest-Litovsk

Kursk

Voronezh

POLAND

Kiev

Kharkov

Stalingrad

Rostov-on-Don

HUNGARY

Kishinyov

Odessa

ROMANIA

Sevastopol

BULGARIA

TURKEY

| | Front line December 1941 |
| --- | --- |
| | Front line October 1942 |
| | Front line July 1943 |
| | Front line June 1944 |

0        200

# Foreword
### *by Tim Renton, M.P.*
### *Minister of State at the Foreign and Commonwealth Office*

As our dialogue broadens with the new regime in Moscow, a key question is whether the Soviet attitude to the human rights of all those who do not conform to their system is going to change. This question is of vital importance to the different groupings in the Soviet Union who have for the last seventy years found themselves in the bear's hug of a Marxist/Leninist revolution that was incapable of taking into account their individual beliefs.

We are all delighted when a well-known individual like Orlov is released or when the campaign to free the Christian poetess, Irina Ratushinskaya, from her sentence of hard labour is successful. But it is a hard fact that for everyone released following the work of ardent campaigners, there are a hundred thousand who remain confined, either literally in a camp or hospital or mentally in spiritual bondage. One swallow does not make a summer.

The Soviet leaders are now showing themselves willing to discuss humanitarian issues. Gorbachev is not Krushchev, Shevardnadze is not Gromyko. The aim for the Westerner – be he priest, politician or tourist – who comes in contact with the Soviets must be to remind them always of their duty to open up their country in terms of allowing religions to flourish, unorthodoxy to be acceptable and exit visas for all those who wish to leave. The next few years could mark a crossroads; the signposts are not clear.

Gerald Buss has thus done a very timely service in

writing this important history of religious believers in the Soviet Union, and their relationship with the State since the Revolution. He reminds us very fully of the weight of Soviet law against dissenters and of the continual threat of harassment against those whose only crime is to have attended a registered church.

At a time when human rights are being so extensively discussed at the Vienna conference, that is a follow-up to the Helsinki Final Act, it is essential that the West should be reminded of the awful prison conditions in the Soviet Union, the barbarity of the labour camps and the misuse of forceable confinement in psychiatric hospitals. The details listed by Mr Buss chill the marrow in our bones.

But how pleased Airey Neave would be that this work should have been helped on its way by a scholarship funded under his memorial trust. Dedicated as he was to the concept of freedom within the law, his trustees must be delighted that Gerald Buss has produced such an erudite examination of the loss of freedom for religious believers in the Soviet Union. Irina Ratushinskaya writes in one of her poems:

> For the cry from the well of 'mama!'
> For the crucifix torn from the wall,
> For the lie of your 'telegrams'
> When there's an order for an arrest –
> I will dream of you, Russia.

These are moving lines, and Gerald Buss has collected all the facts and sad history that lie behind them.

*Tim Renton,*
*November 1986*

# Preface

*by Michael Bourdeaux*
*Founder and General Director of Keston College*

Gerald Buss had produced a valuable addition to the available literature on the Suffering Church. He brings together many sources in a readable and compact way. The strength of the book is its organisation and selection, which makes it an admirable volume to be put in the hands of those who know little of the subject. Within that category come the vast majority of not only lay people, but also clergy right up to leadership level.

Every Christian visitor to the Soviet Union should know what *The Bear's Hug* contains and careful reading of it will enhance the experience beyond measure.

The author tackles the central contradiction which is so difficult for the outsider to reconcile. The visitor sees magnificent open churches and can participate in worship which wells up from elemental springs; he can attend peace conferences and meet Soviet church leaders who, included in the warmth of their welcome, reiterate assurances that there is no religious persecution today. Yet, at the same time, that visitor may well have been briefed by Keston College that there are hundreds of religious prisoners and that there are whole groups of Christians, as well as Jews, who feel that their only future is to emigrate – if only permission were forthcoming.

*The Bear's Hug* explores this duality and illustrates how the two faces, though contradictory, are actually both part of the full picture and must be held together in focus if any correct judgment is to be made.

Russian Orthodox church history, the main outlines of Soviet legislation on religion and its application in practice, the nature of Government controls, the Soviet Union's signing of international agreements on religious liberty, the life-style of an ordinary believer: these diverse subjects are clearly expounded and interlace in a logical whole.

Once again, the underlying question urges itself to the forefront of the reader's mind: is it possible that this super-power can ever become a model of civilization or play its full role in world development while it adheres to its self-mutilating policy of militant atheism? Believers could make an immense contribution to all aspects of Soviet life and the vitality and enduring quality of religious experience there makes it certain that one day they will. Gerald Buss provides practical guidance and wisdom on how Christians elsewhere can and should involve themselves practically in working towards this end.

*Michael Bourdeaux,*
*Keston College,*
*October 1986*

# 1

# Introduction

The Russian Orthodox Church has a particular fascination for many of us living in the West. It seems to embody all that is most truly Russian. At the same time there are conflicting and confusing accounts of what is happening under the Soviet Government not only to the Orthodox Church but to believers generally. At the very time that the Russian Orthodox Church was hosting a huge international peace conference in Moscow in May 1982, the "Siberian Seven" (Pentecostal Christians) were taking refuge in the United States Embassy in Moscow for the fifth successive year. They were living in one room, after applying to the Soviet authorities for visas to leave the USSR simply because they were unable to practise their faith freely.

We hear a good deal about the persecution of the Church in Russia and the harassment of believers. Some are sentenced to prison, others sent to camps, or into exile thousands of miles away within the Soviet Union; others again are confined to psychiatric hospitals, unable even to be brought to trial but condemned as insane. Here is one aspect of religious life in the USSR then – one that is well supported by evidence and is true. But it is only one side of the coin.

The other side of the coin is equally true, and brought home in a dramatic way to anyone visiting the Soviet Union for the first time and going to a church. The first thing that may take him aback is that it is possible to go to church at all. He may also be surprised to know that there is a choice, at any rate in the major cities like Moscow and Leningrad. Indeed if he wants to go to church all he need do is ask the Intourist guide, or take a taxi, and he will have no trouble in finding a church. It is all quite above board, and the guide will tell you that churches are open and that religion is free in the Soviet Union. On his return home, such a visitor may well ask what all the fuss is about, and say like a member of the first party I took to the USSR: "We went to church perfectly freely, and it was packed with worshipping Russians. I thought you told us that the Church was persecuted in the USSR. We could not see any evidence of it at all".

Indeed any visitor going to church in Russia will encounter a remarkable scene: a church that is open and full, services of quite incredible beauty, which will continue for anything up to three or four hours, and a congregation of perhaps thousands, who are fully participating, venerating the icons, or standing transfixed in ascetic devotion. By all appearances there is freedom of worship, and believers can come and go as they wish. A visitor may therefore be excused for coming away with the impression that all is basically well with the Church in Russia, and that the talk of persecution is exaggerated. After all, where do you experience such large numbers and such devotion in the West?

There is another aspect of the picture which is confusing too. Occasionally in our daily papers we see pictures of bearded Russian Orthodox bishops arriving in the West on official delegations and being received at Lambeth Palace by the Archbishop. These churchmen are apparently able to travel out of the Soviet Union without any trouble, and give the impression when asked that persecution does not exist. What is the truth? They are the leaders of the Russian Church, so surely they must know what is going on? Perhaps, we think, we have got the wrong picture. Similarly, Western churchmen go regularly to the USSR and are extremely well received. However, many return confused as well as fascinated by the experience; few feel they have been able to discover what exactly is going on.

Thus the question that this book sets out to answer is, what is the real situation of believers in the Soviet Union? We know that both sides of the coin present true pictures, but how do we resolve the contradictions? The book aims to speak not to the expert or to those who have lived under Communist rule, but to ordinary people who are genuinely confused by what they hear and see. It seeks to iron out some of the confusions which exist in their minds.

Why, though, should the predicament of the Church in Russia be so important anyway? Does it really matter what happens to believers? Here there are three main things to be said.

First, the Soviet Union is a one-party state. There is no legal alternative to the Party. The only institutions which are not directly inspired and run by the Party are, in fact, religious bodies. The Churches are in a peculiar position: they have no place in law as institutions, but paradoxically are allowed to exist and are not essentially under Party control. As such they are of high potential importance for any future social or political evolution within the USSR.

Second, believers in the Soviet Union present valuable lessons to us in the West. Certainly there are tensions for any believer trying to live out his faith in the West, tensions more often than not brought about by the conflict between faith and our materialistic society; but it is especially informative to learn how believers survive when living under conditions similar to those of the early Church. To discover this it is necessary to examine the laws which govern religious activity in the Soviet Union, as well as to look at what actually happens to believers. Is it possible, for example, for totalitarianism and Christianity to live side by side with each other? Or is it inevitable that a Soviet State has to persecute religion?

And third, such a study is important from an ecumenical point of view. It is part of our duty as believers to learn how other Christians live in different parts of the world, and to show our support for them as part of the universal Church.

Nowhere is this more important than in a country beset by persecution.

This book would never have got started without the ready help and assistance of Keston College, who specialise in the study of religious communities in the Soviet Union and Eastern Europe. The staff gave me free access to their activities, and much of the material quoted on harassment and imprisonment of believers, as well as case studies, is taken from their records. I am particularly grateful to Dr Philip Walters, the Research Director of Keston College, who has put up with a continual barrage of questions and read and corrected my text without complaint; as well as to Michael Rowe, Head of Soviet research, and Malcolm Walker, librarian and archivist at the College.

I am also grateful to the Airey Neave Memorial Trust for their generous scholarship, which has enabled me to travel and research widely. I hope that they will feel that this book will stand as a further tribute to the memory of Airey Neave, who fought so bravely to maintain freedom under the law in many countries.

I should also like to thank Patrick Miles for all his help and enthusiastic support, and for his continual encouragement extended over a number of years. I remain indebted to the Master and Fellows of Corpus Christi College, Cambridge for allowing me to carry out my research as a Fellow Commoner of the College; as well as to the Governors, Headmaster, Staff and boys of Hurstpierpoint College for giving me the time and courage to undertake this task. I am grateful to Mrs Elizabeth Kennedy for her translation of the Furov document.

Finally, I am much beholden to my wife Vivian, and my daughters Celina, Sofie and Chloe. Without their patience and indulgence this book would have been abandoned long ago, and they might have seen more of me.

# 2

# The Russian Orthodox Church 1917–1943

On the eve of the 1917 revolution the Russian Orthodox Church was a substantial institution. It had 117 million members, with 130 bishops and 48,000 functioning churches. There was a total of 50,000 clergy of all ranks. The Church ran 35,000 primary schools and 58 seminaries. However, the Church was closely identified with the Tsarist state and had been subject to strict bureaucratic control for two hundred years.

Peter the Great had in effect made the Church little more than a department of state headed by a secular bureaucracy appointed by the Tsar himself. In exchange for their loyalty bishops lived in luxury, but were captives of the State with their administrative authority severely restricted even in purely religious matters. The office of Patriarch had been suspended and in its place a synod of bishops, selected by the Tsar, was declared to be the supreme organ of government in the Russian Orthodox Church. In reality the synod was a state organ. The bishops were allowed to discuss only those issues which were presented to them by the lay Procurator of the Synod, who in practice ran the Church. Priests depended for a living on donations from parishioners, and added to their meagre income by farming plots of land alongside the peasants. They were isolated from the hierarchy of the Church and were often unpopular with their parishioners, who regarded them as an economic burden. Added to this, the parish priest was expected to act as a source of information for the State on local difficulties and to report on anything that might threaten the interests of the State. This in itself helped destroy the sacred bond of trust between the priest and his people; a situation that was naturally resented by many Orthodox Christians. Many of the intellectual class were completely alienated from the Church; others, including many churchmen, began to demand reforms.

The 1905 Revolution provided the first real opportunity for the restoration of the Church's independence. Nicholas II granted toleration to non-Orthodox religions and under pressure issued an Imperial decree promising to convoke a sobor (council). Representatives of the Church were called together and a commission prepared a programme. A thorough reconstruction of the entire ecclesiastical structure was recommended. However, by 1907 reaction had again set in without the Orthodox Church having been allowed to convene a sobor at all. It can fairly be said, that the established Church was in a rather worse position than other christian denominations at that time. Since 1905 the latter had been allowed to meet and discuss, and were not bound by the ties of a restrictive state machine. The clergy of the Russian Orthodox Church, on the other hand, were as powerless as before, having failed to win independence from the State. The Church was again stifled and continued to be so until 1917. This situation was particularly aggravated in the last years before the Revolution when many bishops were men personally recommended by Rasputin.[1]

In February 1917, when the Empire collapsed, the Church found itself without a proper constitution and with all the disadvantages of a body which had been deprived of independence for centuries. It was obvious that a Council had to be summoned as soon as possible. But conditions were not at all favourable. Part of European Russia lay in German hands, and public disorder began to increase after the abdication of the Tsar. Many thought it too late to reconstruct the Church, but the leaders were determined to do all they could. The trouble was that after the removal of the Tsar and without a Patriarchal head the Church lacked the organisational means to become a self-ruling institution.

Nevertheless, many churchmen were glad to see the Tsar go. His abdication was thought by them to be "the hour of general freedom for Russia; the whole land . . . rejoiced over the bright new days of its life".[2] The Provisional Government was generally welcomed. The new Government allowed a sobor to be called, and on 15 August 1917 an impressive gathering of 564 church members took place in the Cathedral of St Saviour in Moscow. Each of the seventy-two dioceses sent its bishop as well as two priests and three laymen. Representatives came from the missions, monastic communities, universities, and theological academies – as well as from the Duma (parliament). The Council (sobor) included 350 laymen. The spirit of quiet industry which characterised the Council contrasted sharply with the growing disorder in the country at large.

One major issue which divided the Council was that of how the Church should be led. The majority, including the laity, wanted to restore the Patriarchate, the traditional form of church government, but a large number of parish clergy were opposed to this. Once again the old rivalry between the "white" clergy, who were married, and the "black" unmarried monastic clergy, began to show itself. The white clergy feared that the black clergy, from whose ranks the bishops were drawn, would dominate the Church, and in so doing reduce still further the influence of the parish priest.

It was while the Council was still in session that the Bolsheviks under Lenin seized power in St Petersburg. However, the Council continued its debate, and a vote was taken on 31 October when it was decided to restore the Patriarchate. There were three main contenders for the office: Antony, Metropolitan of Kiev, a conservative; Bishop Arseniy; and Bishop Tikhon, the recently elected Presiding Bishop of the Moscow Diocese. As none of the three gained an overall majority lots were drawn and

Bishop Tikhon was chosen, in spite of having received fewer votes in the original ballot. The new Patriarch was enthroned in the Cathedral of the Dormition in the Kremlin on 21 November 1917 by special permission of the Bolsheviks, who had recently captured this area of Moscow and placed it under their control. The ceremony was marred only by the damaged state of the cathedral, which had had its dome pierced by shellfire.

After the election of the Patriarch the Council continued its work energetically and plans for the regeneration of the Church were quickly drawn up. A new constitution laid down that the supreme organ of the Russian Orthodox Church was to be the Council, composed of bishops, priests, and laity, and responsible to the Patriarch. A synod of bishops and a council of elected representatives were added to help him carry out his duties. The Council also wanted to revive parish life and strengthen missionary work, as well as reorganise schools. The Council ended its discussions in August 1918. Perhaps one of its most important decrees was to stipulate that the Church would maintain a strictly neutral position in politics. Believers could hold their own opinions, but none was to commit the Church to any particular system.

Unfortunately, none of the sobor's proposed reforms was put into effect, because once the Bolsheviks had consolidated their power they launched a fierce attack against the Church. However, this Council was of great historical importance. It succeeded in uniting the Russian Orthodox Church and gave it a Patriarch who would act as a symbol in a new and violent age.

In spite of the fact that the Church had declared itself to be non-political, Lenin acted to curb its influence immediately. Between December 1917 and the end of January 1918 all church land and property were nationalised, and the State withdrew financial support. The registration of births, marriages and deaths, previously carried out by the Church, was secularised. On 23 January 1918 the important "Decree On the Separation of the Church from the State and of Schools from the Church" was published. In many ways this might have been good news for the Church, because in theory at least from now on it was able to make its own decisions and be responsible for its own affairs. But in practice the Decree meant that the Church was not to have the status of a legal person and so could not in future acquire property. All property required for religious purposes had to be leased from the State, and once leased the building was subject to regular taxes levied on any private enterprise.

In other words, the Church no longer had any control over its buildings. Places of worship which had belonged to it for centuries became the property of the State, together with the ornaments and gifts given over the years by the faithful. Moreover, all bank accounts belonging to religious associations were nationalised, and religion could no longer be taught in schools whether state or private. On the basis of this decree some six thousand churches and monastic buildings were confiscated from the Russian Orthodox Church as having some special historical interest. The cathedrals within the Kremlin long used for crowning the Tsars and the seat of the Patriarch were taken. At the same time, the actual powers of the clergy were reduced, because from now on only groups of laymen were to be recognised as being legally able to lease a church building. The role of the clergy, including bishops, was interpreted as being to retain a spiritual authority over the faithful but no more than that. Indeed a decree published on 13 June 1921 declared that it was illegal to preach a sermon on any theme except of a purely religious nature. Government ownership of church buildings allowed the authorities to close churches in subtle ways. For example, they might agree to let the church building out to the Church on certain days, while allowing the same building to be used as a dance hall or a club on other occasions. This infuriated believers who refused to use a church that had been desecrated in this way. The authorities could then close the church for "lack of interest".

This outlines the situation which faced the Russian Orthodox Church within months of the Bolshevik takeover. How much opposition was there to these measures? At the start some believers were sympathetic to the new regime, and were by no means totally opposed to an alteration in the position of the Church within the State. Yet many people did object to the way the Bolsheviks gained power. The coup of October was regarded as the overthrow of a more or less representative government by a highly organised armed minority. Moreover, this minority was committed to establishing atheism. It was natural that opposition to the new government began to grow within the Church as persecution set in.

As early as 19 January 1918 Patriarch Tikhon published an encyclical condemning the Soviet Government's anti-Church activities and its persecution and terror campaigns against believers. He excommunicated the Bolsheviks with the words: "the commandments of Christ – to love one's neighbour – are forgotten and trampled under foot. Every day there comes to us news of horrible and cruel massacres, the victims of which are innocent men and even people lying on a bed of pain, guilty only of having accomplished in all honesty their duty towards their country".[3]

In its turn the State began to accuse churchmen of acting with political (i.e. anti-Bolshevik) motives. Between 1918 and 1920 twenty-eight bishops were murdered, thousands of priests were imprisoned or murdered, and 12,000 laymen were reported killed for religious activities. By 1920 a total of 673 monasteries had been dissolved out of the 1,025 in existence in 1914. It could be said that "the black clergy were scattered over the face of Russia like cockroaches swept out from under the stove by the hand of a tidy housewife".[4] Some of them joined collective farms, others continued in the underground Church. Yet others wandered about preaching that the Anti-Christ had come. The Patriarch himself was not arrested, but had to be protected day and night by volunteer guards of the faithful. He was deprived of his ration card as a "bourgeois parasite". On 25 September 1919 he issued an encyclical ordering his clergy once again to stand above politics; freeing them from political obligations on the grounds that Church and State were now legally separated.

The years 1920 and 1921 brought unprecedented famine to Russia. The country was still in the grip of civil war, and grain surpluses had been used up. Drought struck the food-growing areas and posed a great threat to the new regime, which had come to power promising amongst other things to feed the people. These famine conditions led to further friction between the Patriarch and the Bolsheviks. In August 1921 Patriarch Tikhon appealed to the Churches to aid the victims of famine. Simultaneously, a National Ecclesiastical Committee was set up to help the starving and collections were made in every church. The Government closed this committee down and appropriated the money for its own Famine Relief Committee. Then on 19 February 1922 the Patriarch ordered all church valuables not used for sacramental worship to be handed over to aid the starving. This order was rebuffed by the Government, who issued their own edict demanding that *all* valuables be handed over including those used for sacramental purposes. The Patriarch responded by refusing to hand over the sacramental objects, yet at the same time urging believers to be generous to the famine victims.[5] This controversy gave the Government a reason to begin a further terror campaign against the Church, misrepresenting it as a heartless institution indifferent to human need. This design is well illustrated by a secret internal order of 22 February 1922, signed by Lenin himself: "At the next Party Congress a secret session should be organised jointly with the leading members of the GPU (predecessor to the KGB), the Commissariat of Justice and the Revolutionary Tribunal. A secret decision of the Congress should approve a mercilessly resolute confiscation of church valuables. The more members of the reactionary bourgeoisie we manage to shoot the better. It is precisely now that we must give such a lesson to these characters that they would not dare to think of any resistance for at least the next few decades. Lenin (Top Secret. No copies to be made)".[6]

There was, of course, great resistance to the removal of church valuables, and the Government was able to use the famine to force a confrontation with the Church, culminating in the arrest of the Patriarch on 10 May 1922. Purges and imprisonment of churchmen became an everyday occurrence. It is estimated that between 1921 and 1923 as many as 2,691 married priests, 1,962 monks, 3,447 nuns, and an unknown number of laymen and women were physically "liquidated".[7]

Yet there was a positive side to all this suffering. The Church, now freed from all state ties for the first time in four hundred years, entered a period of spiritual recovery. To quote one witness: "Sisterhoods appeared in all parish churches. They preoccupied themselves with charity, especially for the imprisoned clergy . . . the church was becoming a state within a state . . . The prestige and authority of the imprisoned clergy was immeasurably higher than that of the clergy under the Tsars".[8] Much *samizdat* was published, and even Soviet authors recognised that "at least since 1923 there was felt a rise in religiosity throughout the country". A contemporary correspondent from Russia wrote that the urban churches were fuller than before the Revolution, with a higher proportion of intelligentsia, many of whom had been converted to Christianity after the Revolution. It should be noted that this revival did not affect the rural areas.

Why was there this resurgence of interest in religion? It could in part have been brought about by a loss of faith in the promised materialistic utopia. Certainly there had been a general decline in the quality of life in Russia as a result of the prolonged civil war. Another factor was that the Church, officially freed from the State, now offered the only legally existing alternative ideology to official Marxism-Leninism.

In every age it is difficult for Christians to know how far they should go in loyalty to the State. The situation for a Church faced with an avowedly atheistic regime is even more difficult. Does it keep quiet and attempt to work for change from within the system, or step outside the system and risk total annihilation as an institution? Such was the dilemma which faced the hierarchy and many believers in the early 1920s. Inevitably, after the civil war splits began to show themselves in the Russian Church along these lines.

How was the Church to deal with these new circumstances? The history of the different factions is long and complicated and this is not the place to examine them in detail. A word must be said, however, about the Living Church or Renovationist movement, which began as an opposition movement within the Orthodox Church and challenged the "anti-Soviet" stand of the clergy. Many Living Church members had been associated before the Revolution with movements for reform both inside and outside the Church, and they certainly had a valid point of view. The difficulty was that they became adopted by the Soviets, who hoped to make the Living Church their officially approved substitute for the Patriarchal Orthodox Church, dedicated to supporting Soviet policy.

We have seen how Patriarch Tikhon was arrested in May 1922 for alleged "anti-Soviet activity". And at that time the Living Church staged a coup in an attempt to become the officially accepted Church. Many Orthodox clergy supported the Living Church, including Metropolitan Sergi (the future Patriarch), and it spread its control over many dioceses. Many clergy loyal to the Patriarchal Church were arrested. Thus now there were two Orthodox Churches in Russia: the Patriarchal Orthodox Church, and the Living Church. This latter enjoyed the total support of the Soviets, which largely accounted for its initial success. It is said that some of its members were also members of the GPU (secret police). Yet others were undoubtedly sincere people inspired only by the highest ideals and motives. For its part, the Government was probably hoping to give the outside world the impression that not all religious institutions were persecuted in the Soviet Union, while at the same time promoting schism and confusion within the Church itself. The year 1923 saw the triumph of the Living Church over the Patriarchal Church; but also the start of its decline. The trial of Patriarch Tikhon had been delayed many times, and on 16 June 1923 he recanted his earlier anti-Soviet stand and said that he would no longer interfere in the politics. As a result of this he was released, and began to issue decrees against the Living Church, and at the same time to urge loyalty to the Soviet Government. Many now left the Living Church and its influence began to decline steadily. In fact the Living Church had never really gained the affections of the believing masses who remained indifferent or even hostile, and paradoxically this lack of popular support must have been a major factor in the Soviet Government withdrawing its support from it. It was finally suppressed in 1943 following the Russian Orthodox Council.

Patriarch Tikhon died on 7 April 1925 and was succeeded as locum tenens by Metropolitan Sergi (Stragorodsky). In 1927 he issued a declaration of Loyalty to the Soviet Government, in which he declared that "the Soviet Union is our civil homeland, whose joys and successes are our joys and successes".[9] This seemed to many believers to go too far in support of the Soviets. How could the Church and an atheistic state have any interests in common, they asked? And so it was that this led to fresh divisions within the Church. Many decided to practise their faith underground. The underground Church or, as it is sometimes called, the Catacomb Church, still exists today, although little is known of its activities. After 1927 it refused to recognise the authority of the Patriarchal Church. Sergi's aim had been to show that it was possible to be at the same time a dedicated Orthodox Christian, and remain loyal to an atheistic state. However it soon became obvious that the Soviet Government was not going to give the Church a chance to demonstrate its loyalty because the most important Soviet law on religion was passed in 1929. It is still basically in force today. It defines as the only legal activity for religious believers that of worshipping in a registered building. All other activities were made illegal or actively discouraged. The only legally recognised religious organisation became the *dvadtsatka*, or group of twenty members. Thus none of the administrative, educational and publishing organisations of the church have any legal status.

It can be truthfully said that "on taking power, the Bolsheviks immediately declared war on the Church. This was probably the only honest act in their whole political activity, for because of the contradictions that separate them, there can be no agreement between these two camps. What dealings can there be between Christ and Satan?"[10]

In fact the Government's attempts to eradicate the Church varied in severity over the years. We have already seen how religion in the early 1920s was strong in spite of intense pressure. At this time the bishops were by and large popular and travelled among their people. Many parishes had at least one priest or preacher who could expound the faith. Life was by no means easy for believers, but it was possible to practise the faith. This became far more difficult in the 1930s, when Stalin attempted something new, namely the physical destruction of the Church as an institution. This onslaught was quite unrelated to the laws of 1929 or any other legality.

By 1940 the situation of the Church was catastrophic. On 22 August 1941 the official publication *Soviet War News* quoted the following statistics. In 1917 there had been 47,457 Orthodox churches, 50,960 Orthodox priests, and 130 bishops. By 1941 there were only 4,225 churches, 5,665 priests and 28 bishops. These figures, however, include the Living Church as well as the newly acquired areas in Eastern Europe. We can assume that the real figure for open churches on pre-1939 Soviet territory was under 1,000, and possibly much lower. And only four bishops remained in Sergi's jurisdiction. In Leningrad only five churches remained open out of 300. The clergy had suffered a similar fate. Reliable sources say that about 42,000 Orthodox clergy were killed between 1918 and the late 1930s.[11]

This general lack of priests was well illustrated by the fact that Odessa, with a population of half a million, had only one open church and no permanent priest. It has been said that this one functioning church was merely a concession to Stalin's eye surgeon Academician Filatov who was a believer. Yet even this church was subject to enormous pressure. Each Sunday a priest would show up to celebrate the Liturgy, only to be arrested next day by the NKVD. The story goes that after all the available priests had dared martyrdom the services were taken by deacons, until they too disappeared; then by psalmists, who would also be liquidated. In the months before the German occupation there remained only laymen who prayed as best they could.[12]

Meanwhile, as in earlier persecutions, the faith did not die. As the churches were closed down, ordinary people remained believers and continued to want the sacraments. The few remaining registered priests, in order to satisfy a fraction of the religious needs of the population, and to protect them from persecutions for attending a church, began to practise mass baptisms, funeral services in absentia on the basis of a message from a believer, and confession by correspondence. Even baptisms and marriages were performed by some priests without the baby or couple being present.[13] Many believers joined the Catacomb Church. These catacomb Christians were not registered, and led a much more spiritually intensive life than the official part of the Church, which was severely controlled and curbed by the authorities. In their secrecy they were able to see to it that their children were brought up in the faith, which the members of the official Church were unable to do.

One of the best examples of this is Father Alexander Men, who is one of the most outstanding priests of the contemporary Moscow Patriarchal Church. He had been baptised and spiritually educated by catacomb priests near Moscow in the 1940s. Father Men did not see the Catacomb Church as a total break with the official Church, but as a comprehensive term for all unofficial and thus uncontrolled church activity. By far the largest part of the Catacomb Church never formally broke with Metropolitan Sergi, but had gone underground because of the impossibility of performing rites openly. However, it was this Catacomb Church who helped save the official Church from complete destruction, because the Soviets were afraid to force the entire Church underground and risk losing control of it.

In the 1930s many clandestine monastic communities appeared to take the place of monasteries closed by the Government. Some were in the depths of Siberian forests, others in cities. "Dispersed monks and nuns often organised Kolkhozes and Sovkhozes",[14] which were in reality a continuation of their monastic communities. Professor Krypton, a former catacomb Christian, described a secret convent in a Leningrad flat: "The services and even the singing were whispered. The organisation had several branches in the city".

Dimitry Pospielovsky tells the extraordinary story about a certain Bishop Peter who had been clandestinely ordained by Patriarch Tikhon. On returning from prison in 1936 he went into a secret dugout where he lived with a few disciples. The NKVD (Peoples Commissariat of Internal Affairs) began a hunt for him in 1937, interrogating hundreds of people, yet could not discover him, although he was in contact with many believers across the country. In 1943, when the situation of the Church had improved, he left the Tien-Shan mountains where he had established an unofficial monastery with some three hundred secretly tonsured monks. The community recognised Sergiy, and survived until 1951 when it was spotted by helicopter. All the monks were imprisoned, while Bishop Peter either died or was killed in prison.[15]

The fact remains that by the outbreak of war in 1941 the visible face of the Church in Russia had all but disappeared.

Metropolitan Sergi must have wondered when, if ever, the Government would accept his and his Church's professed loyalty to the Soviet State, as expressed in his Declaration of 1927, which he had so much hoped would win the Orthodox Church a recognised place in Soviet society. He is quoted as saying in May 1941: "Formerly they used to strangle us, but at least they fulfilled their promises. Now they continue to strangle us, but they no longer fulfil the promises they gave while strangling us".[16]

The Second World War began with the Soviet Union and Nazi Germany in alliance. On 22 June 1941 Hitler broke the Non-Aggression Pact and invaded the Soviet Union. It is reported that Stalin remained in a state of shock for a week before addressing the nation. The first to speak out was Metropolitan Sergi, who on the day of the invasion, which was also the Feast of All the Saints of Russia, wrote a pastoral letter to his parishes telling them to remain loyal to the Motherland. Part of the letter read: "Our Orthodox Church has always shared the destinies of the Nation . . . together with it it has borne both trials and successes. Neither shall she abandon her people today". Sergi was hoping that Stalin would now realise he needed the Church and would become more lenient in his dealings with it. The Metropolitan continued to take every opportunity to express his full support for the Government, declaring: "progressive humanity has declared a holy war against Hitler in the name of Christian civilization, for freedom of conscience and religion".[17]

During the first phase of the war the Germans occupied a large part of European Russia with a population of about eighty million people. They acted with considerable tolerance towards religion in these areas. Perhaps the idea was to use these conquered Slavs to help defeat the Bolsheviks. The head of the Ostministerium, Alfred Rosenberg, worked out German policy on religion during a meeting with Hitler on 8 May 1942, and in June issued a "Toleration Act". The Nazis had realised that the best way to guarantee the support of the general population was to allow them freedom to practise their religious faith.

The extent of the religious revival under the Nazis is evident from the experiences of a mission sent to the northern areas around Pskov and Novgorod in 1941. The missionaries found very few churches open when they arrived, and reopened about three hundred. They baptised many children and reported enormous enthusiasm for religion among the local people. One report said: "When we arrived in Pskov, parishioners with tears in their eyes approached us in the streets for our blessing. At the first service all the worshippers confessed, 'it was not the priests who had come to strengthen the people, the people were there to strengthen the priests'".[18] In fact 40% of the total population of Pskov (10,000 out of 25,000) participated in the ceremony of the Blessing of the Water on the Feast of the Epiphany in January 1942. Three thousand five hundred children were baptised between August and November 1941. Many teachers who had taught atheism in the schools became members of the Church. The German reports speak of the great success of the Pskov Mission and tell how almost all the population turned out for church services. Another report said: "the religiousness of the population is so strong that it is possible to tear the Russian people away from the Soviet Government by relying simply on that".[19] In fact by the end of the German occupation there were 175 priests serving 200 parishes, and they relied for money entirely on the generosity of parishioners.

The religious revival in the occupied areas had no parallel in the part of the country which remained under Soviet control. Indeed no opportunity was given for the Church to revive, in spite of all Sergi's declarations of loyalty and protestations of support for the Government. Evidently his actions had not really won him the trust of the Soviets. As the German armies advanced towards Moscow the Metropolitan was moved east to Ulyanovsk ostensibly to protect him as leader of the Russian Church, but with the effect of preventing him being captured by the Germans in the event of Moscow falling, and then being used as an anti-Soviet tool.

The grim situation of the Orthodox Church in the home-land was in sharp contrast to that of the Church in Belorus-sia, which was under German occupation. By 1941 the devastation of the Church in this region by the Soviet regime had been almost total. For example, in Minsk out of seventeen churches, a monastery and a convent, none remained open in 1937. Yet within four months of the German occupation seven churches had reopened and were full, and 2,200 infant baptisms were carried out. Out of 400 pre-revolutionary churches in the Minsk Diocese, 120 were reopened in the first year of the German occupation.

The situation in the Ukraine was different and more complicated, because the national leaders were Catholic – a Church which the Nazis were less inclined to support. In spite of this there was an enormous religious revival which in part reflected Ukrainian nationalism. According to Ger-man reports as many as 70%–90% of the population came back to the Church. There are reports of full churches, a shortage of priests, mass baptisms, and mass church weddings. In the two years of German occupation large numbers of churches were reopened.

There is, then, plenty of evidence that after twenty-three years of persecution and intensive atheistic education, religion far from being destroyed had actually grown in strength. An interesting comment is made by Father Nikolai Trubetskoi, a priest from the Pskov Mission who after the war served ten years in Soviet concentration camps, and who was active in Riga until his death in 1978. "Little has changed since the war", he said. "A similar missionary effort today would produce similar religious zeal and upsurge".[20]

The mass opening of churches in the areas of the Soviet Union occupied by the Germans preceded, and in part prompted, a change of policy by Stalin. First of all the Patriarch was allowed to publish his patriotic addresses: this was possible only on a liberal reading of the law of 1929. Then the Soviet authorities gave permission for the Church to publish a volume called *The Truth about Religion in Russia*. This was aimed at foreign readers, and inevitably contained a good deal of propaganda. The Church was also allowed to open a bank account and to make collections for the defence of the Motherland, a concession which again went beyond the provisions of the 1929 legislation. This new facility was very effective and by the middle of January a large sum had been collected by the faithful for the starving people of Leningrad.

The main and by far the most dramatic change came on 4 September 1943 when Stalin invited the three remaining Orthodox Metropolitans still functioning on Soviet territory to the Kremlin to discuss the future of the Church. There are no detailed accounts of the meeting, but in view of all that had gone before, the persecutions, murders, closure of churches, and the general attack on the Church as well as the total suppression of religious liberty, it is interesting to read what record there is.

"The three Metropolitans were picked up at 9 p.m. on 3 September and whisked to the Kremlin, where they were ushered into Stalin's presence. The only other person present was the Foreign Minister Molotov. Molotov said that the Soviet Government and Stalin would like to know what the needs of the Church were. Sergi told him of the great need to reopen churches as well as seminaries, and that the Church needed also to be allowed to convene a Council. Stalin is reported to have broken in at this point and to have asked the bishops directly: 'Why don't you have cadres, where have they disappeared to?' Everyone of course knew that the cadres had disappeared in the camps. Sergi replied: 'There are all sorts of reasons why we have no cadres. One of the reasons is that we train a person for priesthood, and he becomes a Marshal of the Soviet Union'. Stalin smiled with satisfaction and said: 'Yes of course I am a seminarian'. He began to reminisce about his years in the seminary. They talked until about three in the morning, and it was then that the future statute of the Russian Orthodox Church was drafted. The old Metropolitan Sergiy was absolutely exhausted. Stalin took him by the arm, led him carefully down the stairs and said on parting: 'Your Grace, that is all I can do for you at the present time'."[21]

Within four days a Council gathered. Sergi was elected Patriarch of Moscow and two more Metropolitans were consecrated, while a further six returned from exile. The Church began to regain some degree of normality. The Patriarchate was moved from its log cabin on the outskirts of Moscow into the impressive surroundings of the former German Embassy. Other concessions followed, such as the restoration to the Church in 1945 of the Novodevichy Convent, which was opened as a theological institute. This was later moved to the ancient Holy Trinity St Sergius Monastery of Zagorsk. Churches began to be reopened, and the Patriarchate was allowed to start publishing a regular journal. At the same time considerable restraints still remained upon the Church, and there was a price to be paid. The authorities began to require the leaders and ordinary clergy of various religious bodies in the Soviet Union to help pursue various Soviet foreign policy aims, and to speak out on every possible occasion in support of Soviet political "truth". Meanwhile any spontaneous religious activity or signs of spiritual creativity in the Churches continued to be heavily checked. This is the situation still in force today.

# 3

# The Russian Orthodox Church Since 1943

We saw in the last chapter that 1943 marked a turning point in the fortunes of the Church. Stalin had met the leaders and granted a degree of toleration. Sergi had become Patriarch. In 1943 the Soviet Government also set up a Council for Religious Affairs (CRA) under a layman, G. G. Karpov. He was to negotiate directly with the church leaders. The law of 1929 still remained in force and the Church had no legal position in the State, but this appointment in fact implied some sort of recognition. It also meant that the State could control the Church more easily, and in so doing violate the 1918 Decree on Separation of Church from State. In 1944 Sergi died and was succeeded by Metropolitan Alexi, who was enthroned the following year at a ceremony attended by Orthodox dignitaries from Russia and abroad. The accompanying Council passed a "Statute on the Administration of the Russian Orthodox Church", an essential document now that the Church had *de facto* recognition as a centralised institution.

Thus by 1945 the Church was all but an accepted institution in law, and was even allowed to buy property. The church leaders in return expressed their admiration for Stalin and all he was doing for Russia. On the occasion of Stalin's seventieth birthday on 21 December 1949, for example, a *Te Deum* was sung and in the homily Alexi said: "Stalin is the first amongst the fighters for peace among all the nations of the world . . . he is our leader, whose charming personality disarms any who have met him by his

kindness and attentiveness to everybody's needs . . . by
the power and wisdom of his speech".[1]

From 1943, churches were reopened, and new ones built.
Exact figures are hard to establish, but by all reliable
accounts the number of functioning churches grew to a
maximum of about one half of the pre-revolutionary total of
about 50,000. Estimates of the number of open churches in
1939 after the purges range from under 100 to 4,000, so either
way the number reopened by the mid-1950s was considerable. As early as 1944 the first theological school to be
opened since the 1920s became operative, and a second was
opened in Leningrad the following year. Over the next two
years six more seminaries opened in different parts of the
Soviet Union, and correspondence courses were established for people unable to attend full-time training. These
were nowhere near adequate for the number of priests
needed, but as more offered themselves for training it
became possible to raise the standard of entry, and the
eventual product of these schools improved accordingly.

Why did the Government continue to practise a more
tolerant policy towards the Church? During the struggle
against Germany Stalin needed the loyalty of the Church,
which could claim to represent a quarter of the population,[2]
to help rally the nation to the patriotic cause; but after the
war church leaders began to fear that they would no longer
be of use to the authorities. A new area was opening,
however. As the Soviet Union extended its control in
Eastern Europe, the Russian Orthodox Church was expected to try to consolidate its own leadership in the world
Orthodox community.

Thus it was that Patriarch Alexi travelled to Jerusalem
and the Near East in May 1945 pointedly excluding the
Ecumenical Patriarch from his itinerary. This was especially
offensive because the Patriarch of Constantinople was regarded as the titular leader of the Eastern Church. Meanwhile Alexi and the other hierarchs visiting Eastern Europe
were able to negotiate something of a reunion with other

Orthodox Christians abroad, and persuade them to recognise the primacy of the Moscow Patriarchate. This move was particularly useful to Stalin as it helped bring Eastern bloc countries directly under the influence of Moscow. Alexi hoped to go further and demonstrate the primacy of the Russian Orthodox Church over the Ecumenical Patriarch by holding a pan-Orthodox Conference in Moscow in 1947. He wanted this to be the first Ecumenical Council to be held since the eighth century. Moscow, he argued, was the third Rome. Rome herself had fallen to the barbarians; Constantinople, the second Rome, had fallen to the Turks in 1453; and so it became Moscow's destiny now to rule the Orthodox world. This was not in fact a new claim and had been put forward as early as the sixteenth century. However, it is not surprising that the Ecumenical Patriarch took a very dim view of the idea, and sent his apologies when the invitations were received. Not to be put off, Alexi then invited Orthodox leaders to a different function to celebrate the 500th year of Russian religious self-rule. This took place, but was only partly a success. The statements which came out of the conference tended to reflect Soviet political interests too faithfully. 1948 marked the end of Moscow's bid for leadership of the Orthodox world.

The Russian Church was able to help the Soviet Government in another way. Since the end of the Second World War relations between the Soviets and the Vatican had been cool. The Catholic Church generally adopted a stance of opposition to Soviet power in Eastern Europe after the fighting was over. Stalin intended to try and sever all ties between Catholics and the Vatican in those countries, and chose to launch an attack on the Ukrainian Uniate Church by forcing it to unite with the Russian Orthodox Church. The Uniate Church, formed in the sixteenth century, retained Orthodox rites but was under the jurisdiction of the Vatican. For a long time it had been the cradle of Ukrainian nationalism. By 1951 it had ceased to exist. Quite obviously it was in Soviet interests to ensure reunification, as this helped weld the Ukraine into the Soviet fold. It is very

uncertain whether Alexi was aware of the violence and
repression that accompanied this reunification, but he was
certainly ready to endorse the exercise. In his address to the
Uniates Alexi told them to abandon the influence of the
Vatican and the inhuman face of Hitlerism, and to turn
"into the arms of your true mother the Russian Orthodox
Church".[3]

Although the Russian Church was able to incorporate the
Uniates, she failed to become the accepted leader of Orthodoxy. And by 1948 the Church seemed to have exhausted
its usefulness to Stalin in the field of foreign affairs. By then
Russian expansionism in Europe had reached its turning
point. 1948 was the year of the Berlin blockade and the cold
war began in earnest. Stalin now aimed at retrenchment
and the consolidation of power.

A new role for the Church was now established in the field
of propaganda rather than direct political activity. It was to
promote the idea of "peace" as a Soviet aim in the post-war
world, while at the same time branding the capitalist countries as warmongers. Obviously "peace" as a general aim
could be supported by the Church without hypocrisy, but it
is interesting to see how the so-called "peaceful" Church
was able to mount attacks of enormous belligerence on the
allegedly aggressive capitalists. The Soviet Government
participated in the peace movement from the earliest post-
war days. Several organisations were founded. The best
known is the World Peace Council (WPC), which sought to
promote Soviet interests in that area. The Church gave
active support to this involvement, and in 1949 Metropolitan Nikolai was elected a permanent member of the committee of the World Peace Council. In 1952 the Patriarch
convened a meeting of representatives of all religious
groups in the USSR in the cause of peace.

The Peace Movement was, though, essentially a defensive weapon. In 1948 the Soviet Union was well behind the
USA in weapon technology. Only the USA had the atomic
bomb. It was, therefore, particularly important to make it

known in clear tones that the Soviet Union wanted only peace, and so inhibit Western rearmament as well as the formation of military alliances potentially hostile to the USSR. The Peace Movement also hoped to influence Western non-communist groups like the Churches and pacifist organisations. In this respect the Russian Orthodox Church was especially useful. It could mobilise latent pacific feelings amongst religious groups in the West; and this policy did in fact have a considerable effect. In May 1952, for example, the Peace Conference held in Moscow unanimously supported the promotion of *pax Sovietica* and condemned Western aggression.

The World Peace Council indulged in anti-Western propaganda. The USA was depicted as a potential aggressor with no moral scruples. It was claimed, for example, that the USA was using bacteriological weapons in Korea, which was entirely untrue. Soviet spokesmen at the WPC also exaggerated out of all proportion the racist elements in US foreign policy. At the first Peace Conference held in August 1949 Metropolitan Nikolai called the USA "the rabid fornicatoress of resurrected Babylon . . . who is trying to seduce the World while pushing it further towards war". And during the Korean War he said: "the spirit and the flesh of fascism have not disappeared . . . no sooner had they begun their criminal aggression than the American neo-fascists began the planned, cannibalistic extermination of the 'inferior' Korean race. Executions without trial . . . they cut off ears, noses, and breasts, gouging out eyes, they break arms and legs, crucify patriots, bury women and infants alive . . . they scalp Korean patriots for 'souvenirs' . . . the American criminals first of all slaughtered political prisoners (from 200,000–400,000 people) forcing them to dig their own graves beforehand . . . the barbaric bombing of peaceful towns and villages has been carried out solely for the purpose of annihilating the civilian population".[4] It has been argued that Metropolitan Nikolai was deliberately exaggerating in the hope that his listeners would understand that what he said was not to be believed. Certainly

Soviet citizens are sceptical about propaganda but have to accept it as an inevitable part of Soviet life. Emigrés from the USSR are often surprised to learn how seriously we in the West take such statements.

In the international peace forum the Russian Orthodox Church spokesmen also subscribed to a narrow definition of pacifism and especially Christian pacifism: that a true pacifist was one who agreed with the Soviet Peace Movement. "All religious people must support the appeal of the World Peace Council", they claimed.[5] In this way the Church made a very useful contribution to Soviet foreign policy aims. In the 1950s, after Stalin's death and the subsequent rise of Khrushchev, Soviet foreign policy became somewhat more subtle. The challenge implied in the old Stalinist quip "How many divisions has the Pope?" had given way to the realisation that the Soviet Union needed a good image in the world at large. Here again the Church was useful: it was able to promote the idea that Russia had radically changed since Stalin's death.

A specifically Christian forum for the debate on peace was the Christian Peace Conference (CPC), founded in Czechoslovakia in 1958. This claimed to be the only effective bridge between Christians of East and West. It stood outside the political sphere and attempted to promote peaceful coexistence from a specifically Christian point of view. It regarded itself as of equal status with the World Council of Churches. In its early years the CPC did effective work in encouraging East–West dialogue and its activities bore good results. For example, the American Churches participating in it helped sway US opinion against the Vietnam War. After the Soviet invasion of Czechoslovakia in 1968, however, the CPC became much more obviously the vehicle for representing Soviet policy and its credibility declined.

The international policies of the Russian Orthodox Church followed those of the Soviet Government in other areas. In line with tendencies of Soviet foreign policy, the rift between the Vatican and the Patriarchate was healed after the accession of Pope John XXIII, and relations between the Church and the Ecumenical Patriarch also improved. In 1948 the Russian Orthodox Church had turned down an invitation to join the World Council of Churches (WCC), but after the second assembly of the WCC in 1954 contact was resumed, and the Church finally joined in 1961.

Stalin died in 1953. There was no totally clear outcome to the subsequent power struggle until 1957. In 1954 there was a brief outburst against religion in the so called "Hundred Days Campaign" and a CPSU (Communist Party of the Soviet Union) Central Committee resolution stated that something must be done to halt renewed interest in religion. Local CP and Komsomol committees were to appoint atheistic tutors to believers and visit them at home. If this kind of approach failed to yield results it was to be followed up by harassment at work, or in colleges, appointment to low paid jobs, or expulsion from universities. Pressure was also put on priests to defect from the Church, and about two hundred did. Patriarch Alexi spoke out amidst renewed persecution, pointing out that the Russian Church was the cradle and protector of the Russian way of life, and had always been loyal to the State. Apart from this brief campaign, however, the years 1954–1958 were good years for the Church and there was a fair degree of toleration.

This situation was brought to a decisive end in 1959 with the anti-religious campaign begun by Khrushchev. In 1960 the relatively tolerant head of the Council for Religious Affairs G. G. Karpov was replaced by the more doctrinate V. A. Kuroyedev. At the same time the widely respected Metropolitan Nikolai was released from his duties to die in obscure circumstances the next year. A new era had begun for the Church. It is somewhat ironic that while the Church was doing her utmost to promote the Soviet image abroad, her very existence was once again under threat within the USSR.

Let us pause for a moment to take a look at the number of active priests and open churches in the period between the

Second World War and 1959. It is estimated that the Leningrad Seminary had 320 students in 1952, while the seminary at Zagorsk had between 350 and 400. In 1953 there were an estimated 30,000 priests serving 20,000 parishes. These figures can only act as a rough guide, and it is even more difficult to assess the number of practising believers. The Alexander Nevsky Cathedral in Leningrad had about 400,000 communicants in Lent 1947, and a similar figure was given for the Patriarchal Cathedral in Moscow in 1946. Despite the reopening of churches, relatively few were functioning compared with the period before the revolution. It was also expensive for the Church to maintain the buildings. A state tax was levied on all churches and church employees. Church buildings which had been restored to religious use by the State were often in appalling condition. The historic Novodevichy Convent in Moscow, which was returned to the Church in 1945, needed a new floor in the sanctuary. The iconostasis and altar had to be completely rebuilt. All that remained after ten years of state ownership were the roof and walls. These repairs had to be done at believers' expense. The Cathedral of the Assumption at Vladimir, one of the architectural treasures of Russia, was filled with "mountains of ice and garbage" at the time it was handed back to believers.[6]

What were the reasons for this sudden and ferocious attack in 1959, which caught the Church quite unprepared? In the West Khrushchev had the reputation of being a liberaliser who introduced reform after the terror of the Stalin period. But this was very far from the truth where religion was concerned. For the Russian Orthodox Church the period between 1959 and 1964 was a disaster. Stalin had given the Church a new deal in the Great Patriotic War, and after the war there had followed a period of comparative stability when the Church could re-establish those foundations destroyed in the purges of the 1920s and 1930s. Khrushchev suddenly reversed the situation, using force similar to that used to suppress the Hungarian uprising of 1956. Two main reasons have been put forward. First, Khrushchev's other liberalising moves had brought him criticism from within the Politburo and he needed to show that he was a strong man in some other area. Second, it is suggested that the renewed strength of the Church worried the Government. It could be seen that the Churches offered the only viable alternative doctrine to communism, and there was no doubt that interest in religion was growing rather than declining. In any event Khrushchev regarded Stalin's liberal attitude towards the Church as illegal, and he claimed to be seeking to return to the standards set at the Revolution by Lenin. All Churches were to suffer. If the Russian Orthodox Church seems to suffer more it was because as the "old established" Church it was more prominent.

In response to renewed state pressure the Russian Orthodox Church held a meeting of bishops in 1961 which passed a resolution redefining the role of the parish priest, who in 1945 had been granted administrative power in the parish. He was now deprived of this power, which was handed over to the parish community of at least twenty members, the *dvadtsatka*. In practice this meant to an executive committee of three members, consisting of the Warden, the deputy Warden, and the treasurer, elected by the parish community from amongst the parishioners. Meetings would be held with the permission of the local city or county Soviet. In other words a local Soviet could suspend a meeting and so control the life of the Church when the Soviet's interests conflicted with those of believers. All financial activities, including voluntary contributions paid to the Patriarchate for the upkeep of seminaries, were removed from the supervision of the clergy and handed over to the executive. The priest was to be responsible only for the spiritual leadership of the parish, as well as for the good conduct of the services. This, of course, begged the question. How can a priest be responsible for the moral discipline of his Church when he is not even allowed to take part in meetings of the community or the executive organ?[7]

Khrushchev's administration aimed at restoring Leninist

"Socialist legality": in other words at reducing the Church's position in society to what it had been in the 1920s. Stalin, it was said, had abused Soviet laws on religion so much that by 1945 Church by-laws virtually contradicted the 1929 legislation on Religious Associations, because they made the parish priest master of his parish whereas Soviet law recognised only the *dvadtsatka* as the ultimate authority.

From the point of view of the Church, a parish cannot come into existence without a priest, who has according to canon law always been a member of the local parish community with full rights. The priest always stands at the head of the parish. It is not church property or a place of worship that gives life to the parish but believers; the parishioners of the parish priest. St Matthew Chapter 16 verse 18 clearly points to the authority of the priest over his people. Thus to reduce the parish priest merely to an employee of the *dvadtsatka* was to render the concept "parish" meaningless. Incidently, the granting of ultimate authority to the *dvadtsatka* directly contravenes Soviet legislation on the Separation of Church from State published by Lenin himself.

The onslaught against the Church was very fierce and more direct than the attacks made following the 1917 Revolution and Civil War, although nowhere near as savage as the attacks of 1928–32 and 1937–39. The campaign consisted of two elements: a massive increase in atheist propaganda, and the repression of religious institutions. The authorities were especially anxious to woo young people away from religion. Schools were told to improve their teaching on atheism, and parents were dissuaded from having their children baptised. From now on in order to have a child baptised both parents had to submit their passports, so that the details could be recorded in a register. They then paid a fixed sum of money, and were given an official receipt. These registers were regularly examined by the local authorities to enable them to discover which people had their children baptised and bring pressures to bear on them if necessary. It was precisely to avoid this that some people refused to register baptism, especially as professions like teaching might not be entered by believers. Weddings, funerals, and sick communion in the homes of believers were subject to the same registration procedure. Yet none of this was embodied in the law as such, it was simply obligatory practice introduced at this time. Meanwhile the State had attempted to produce substitute secular ceremonies which it hoped would supersede the church services.

Another important element in Khrushchev's attack on the Church was that the Laws on Religious Associations were to be more rigorously enforced. For example, again with the emphasis on the young, the interpretation of religious instruction to minors was extended to prevent the frequenting of churches by children and young people. No written laws were passed to this effect, but oral instructions by the CRA officials forbidding priests to begin a service in the presence of minors and to give them communion, were complied with by some bishops and many priests.[8] This was accompanied by a press campaign to try to prevent minors from being used as altar boys, under the pretext that this contradicted the laws banning church work for minors.[9] In some instances parents were deprived of parental rights for what the Soviet authorities called the "fanatical religious upbringing" of their children, some of whom were then placed in state boarding schools. A more detailed account of the changes in legislation at this time will be given in Chapter 4.

This new pressure on the Churches affected believers directly. The change of leadership of the CRA was particularly important. From now on the CRA exercised a much tighter grip over church appointments and the general conduct of bishops and priests. This weakened the Church considerably. Parish administration was made totally dependent on the *dvadtsatka*, which was often penetrated by unbelievers or informers. Yet if a priest found an informer in the *dvadtsatka* there was very little he could do. He himself could be removed, or his church deprived of registration and so prevented from operating. The new restrictions on religious activity generally represented an assault on the rights of individual church members, especially the young, who could find themselves unable to advance their careers or get into university.

No really systematic analysis of the affects of Khrushchev's anti-religious campaign has been made, nor are any overall statistics available on the numbers of people affected. We do know, however, that between 1960 and 1964 there was a wholesale closure of churches. The numbers quoted are in the region of 10,000 to 15,000. Few of them have ever been reopened. [10] The number of active churches in 1958 is given at somewhere between 20,000 and 25,000, of which fewer than 8,000 remained open in 1965. Those churches that were still able to function found themselves hedged about by further restrictions. Sermons were censored. Beggars were driven from the churches, and one important way in which the Church could help the poor was thus stopped. Bells, a traditional part of Orthodox worship, could not be rung, preventing the advertising of services. Believers were not allowed to travel on pilgrimages, and no service could be held in the home without special permission. Priests could lose their registration if they took sick communion or heard confession in the homes of believers without CRA consent. These added restrictions made ordinary church life impossible. Priests themselves were sentenced to imprisonment on trumped-up charges, and some were put in psychiatric hospitals. In some cases they were just dismissed and reduced to live like beggars. The files of some clergy imprisoned in the 1930s but later granted amnesty during the Great Patriotic War were reopened for re-examination and some were re-sentenced. Character assassination was a common way of reducing the influence of the clergy amongst their parishioners. Accusations of embezzlement, sexual misdemeanours, collaboration with the Nazis, or simply anti-Soviet activity, could destroy a man's reputation overnight.

The attack upon the monasteries and convents of the Russian Orthodox Church was just as devastating as that on the parishes. The monasteries are the very source of the Orthodox Church's spiritual strength. Great veneration is given to individual monks and nuns, as well as to monasteries which are important places of pilgrimage for the believer. In fact many believers spend a part of their annual holiday in a monastery, which acts as a meeting place where the faithful can exchange views as well as deepen their spiritual conviction. This, of course, is in itself seen as dangerous by the authorities. In the Orthodox Church the monastic life is looked upon as the highest vocation, and so to attack the monasteries is to attack the very heart of Orthodoxy. In 1958 there were sixty-nine monasteries and convents, but by 1964 this number had fallen to ten at the most.[11] There is a great deal of documentation on the closure of monasteries. The Government found it comparatively easy to close them because they have no legal status: Soviet law does not even mention their existence. One monastery which survived, however, was the famous Pochayev Monastery, which the Soviets were forced to leave open because of world-wide publicity given to the pressure brought to bear on it.

The process of liquidation of the monasteries began in 1958 when the 1945 tax exemption on monastic buildings was lifted. From then on the monasteries had to pay an annual land tax, and so had to foot a greatly increased bill just to stay in existence. A decree of the Soviet Council of Ministers of 16 October 1958 ordered a reduction of the land adjacent to monasteries which was used by the monks for food production. No limit was set on the amount of land that could be taken. In the case of Pochayev its agricultural fields and orchards were seized in 1962, in an attempt to starve the 146 monks out of existence. Together with this a secret instruction ordered all local authorities to refuse monastic residence permits to young postulants, with the threat of arbitrary expulsion by the police, imprisonment, or drafting into the armed services for those who resisted. This meant that the monasteries were left with an ageing population of people who were no longer self-sufficient.

As far as Pochayev was concerned, the civil authorities began to requisition the buildings and by 1966 all but the monks' residential building had been confiscated. The hostel for pilgrims was turned into a hospital, and other buildings put to state use. The monastery itself became totally dependent upon the donations of pilgrims, then even these were banned. The authorities' aim was to make the monasteries insolvent, and then to close them for tax evasion. But in this instance the Soviets miscalculated, and by late 1966, after a battle of five years, the harassment and violence ended. The monastery survived, although today it contains only some thirty-five monks.[12] It survived because of the bravery of the monks and local lay people, who were prepared to put up enormous resistance to persecution. They were considerably encouraged in their struggle by pressure from abroad.

Recent information from Russia shows, however, that Pochayev is still under attack by the authorities: we are not recounting old history but contemporary events. The documents show that persecution seemed to have stopped for a while after the Khrushchev period, but that this was a false impression. "Many monks are denied permission to live in the grounds of the monastery", an anonymous report states, "cells stand empty, and Pochayev is on the brink of closure".[13] According to local people the campaign against Pochayev has been carried on since the end of 1983 by both the militia and the KGB. The writer of the report witnessed an incident during a service in the cathedral when militiamen, many in a drunken state, inspected worshippers' documents, and then at the end of the service kicked and beat the people out of the church. A pensioner, the monastery diaryman, was beaten up and later had to go to a psychiatric hospital on the orders of the passport department of the local region, for refusing to leave Pochayev. This, the report says, is not an isolated incident.[13]

One of the effects of the religious persecution of the 1960s was to bring home to religious believers that their "rights" had no legal basis. Khrushchev's anti-religious campaign, endorsed by the twenty-second Party Congress in 1961, did not succeed in destroying religious faith and practice, but it had the effect of driving large sections of the Church underground once more. New practices grew up: prayer by correspondence; funerals *in absentia* after civil burial; weddings *in absentia*; and even confession by correspondence. One Soviet source reported that as many as 63% of all religious rites in one area and 89% in another were performed *in absentia*, in response to requests by letter.[14] Even though it was illegal, many priests would conduct religious ceremonies at home. The most common such ceremony was infant baptism. Another source says that at this time 40% to 60% of all babies in Russia were baptised, which indicated that the number of believers remained high in spite of persecution.[15] Children themselves were skilful at concealing their religious adherence. It was reported, for example, that some children were wearing neck crosses, but that an inspection of 1,000 children by the authorities did not reveal one child wearing a cross. "Some had crosses hanging over their beds at home or on a hook in a closet. Some had one sewn into their pillows, some kept it in a box; only a few wear a cross when they get home from school, or put it on when they go to bed."[16] Another result of Khrushchev's anti-religious actions was the growth of unofficial underground literature. Much of the information coming to the West on the attempts to close Pochayev, for example, arrived in the form of clandestine writings, that is to say "self-published" literature. Bibles and other religious literature were widely circulated in this way. Yet none of this lessens the seriousness of Khrushchev's attack on the institutional life of the Church.

What was the reaction of the Patriarchate, the bishops and the priests to this anti-religious persecution? Although this campaign was short-lived it had its long-term effects. The subservient attitude of the Patriarch in the face of State pressure came to contrast with the determination of a small minority to stand up for believers' rights, and a rift developed between these two groups. In November 1961 Metropolitan Nikodim, who had succeeded Metropolitan Nikolai as the Russian Orthodox representative in foreign affairs, led a delegation to the third General Assembly of the World Council of Churches in New Delhi. He and his companions acted as if everything at home was perfectly normal. The other delegates showed no reaction to the absence of Metropolitan Nikolai, although he was well known to them. He had in fact already been removed from office and died on 13 December. Very few people in the West knew of the renewed persecution of the Russian Orthodox Church and all Christian believers, and an obvious opportunity to publicise these facts was lost.

How did this situation come about? Why did the Patriarch and other Church leaders remain silent? After all the Soviet authorities could with justification have been accused of acting illegally, since they were in violation of their own laws such as the Decree on the Separation of Church from State. Obviously some bishops were well-intentioned and wanted to preserve as much of the institutional Church as possible by remaining silent once the attacks began. Others, even including some in very senior positions, were no doubt silent out of fear for their careers. The following points became clear however. From the start of the campaign the majority of bishops failed to stand up for believers' legal rights, refusing even to appoint successors to those priests who had been removed from office. Reliable sources say that some bishops were actively involved in the closure of churches. Certainly many agreed to the illegal merging of parishes, giving "lack of interest" as the reason. The example of Bishop Ioann of Kirov is interesting. In February 1965 he launched a tirade against a churchwarden, shaking his fists and shouting, "I'll send you off to the NKVD". He closed the churches in his diocese and helped destroy many people's faith. Believers in Kirov wrote to the

Patriarch asking that he be removed. At first no answer was received. Eventually the Patriarch wrote a letter saying that he had no power to appoint or dismiss a bishop; this, he said, was up to the local authority.

Protests were however made against the actions of the authorities. Two of the best known and most important protesters were Father Nikolai Elishman and Father Gleb Yakunin, priests of the Orthodox Church, who decided to put pressure on the Church leadership and the Government through publicity, using the medium of an open letter. They told the World that the Church in the USSR had no rights. This letter, sent on 21 November 1965 to Patriarch Alexi, was the first public statement of the real condition of the Church in the post-Khrushchev period, and it initiated the movement for religious freedom within the Russian Orthodox Church. This movement developed spontaneously alongside the secular human rights campaign, which in fact began simultaneously with the two priests' initiative. On 5 December 1965 a demonstration was held in Moscow under the slogan "Respect your own Constitution". It was organised by the human rights movement, which stood for free speech and legality within the framework of the Soviet Constitution. The Church movement for religious freedom was based on the same principles: free speech and respect for the law.

In their letter the two priests accused the Soviets of breaking Soviet law on the Separation of Church from State, and of interfering in the internal affairs of the Church. They called upon the Patriarch to stand up to the authorities. They also wanted the monasteries and seminaries which had been illegally closed between 1961 and 1964 to be reopened and returned to the Church. Priests must be allowed to hold services in the homes of their parishioners, and children should be allowed to attend church freely. The State must also be prevented from interfering in Church appointments. The reply was swift and came in December. The Patriarch accused the priests of destroying peace and unity within the Church, and of not keeping their ordination vows. He said they were not carrying out their ministry according to ecclesiastical law and under the proper direction of the hierarchy. They were to be removed from their parishes until such time as they repented, but were not defrocked. The laity reacted to this letter, and in June 1966 believers from Kirov headed by Boris Talantov sent an open letter to the Patriarch complaining of the harassment of the Church in their town. Talantov campaigned courageously for religious freedom until his own arrest and death in a labour camp in January 1971.

In April 1970 Patriarch Alexi died at the age of 92. He was succeeded by Metropolitan Pimen of Krutitsy and Kolomna at an open election in the sobor of May/June 1971. Some Russian churchmen have spoken of his excessive fear of the Soviet Government authorities. Archbishop (now Metropolitan) Aleksi of Tallin said that Pimen was a man without will, initiative or administrative talents, lazy and easily influenced by other people's opinions. In this way he was an ideal choice in the eyes of the Soviets.

Accurate figures for those attending church in the 1970s are unobtainable. The State, on the one hand, needed to show a steady decline in church attendance. Diocesan records, on the other hand, are open to CRA investigation and so may well be inaccurate. Figures for 1972 issued by the Patriarchate said that there were 6,850 officially registered churches and 6,180 registered functioning Orthodox priests in the USSR. Khrushchev shut five seminaries, but the three remaining open were able to build in the 1970s, and offer additional courses as well as to add to their number of seminarians. The seminary at Zagorsk, for example, managed to increase its numbers by subterfuge. Repairs were carried out on the buildings, but when the scaffolding was removed in 1980 a new building had appeared. The authorities protested, but to no effect and the seminary keeps the additional space. Three seminaries are not nearly enough to train the number of priests coming forward for ordination, however, and many men are trained outside the institutional framework. The state authorities are prepared to turn a blind eye to unofficial additions to the buildings of seminaries if this means that the number of priests training by correspondence is cut down.

The idea of religious freedom inspired a wide range of unofficial activities by Orthodox believers during the 1960s and 70s. Anatoli Levitin-Krasnov, the Church historian, wrote *samizdat* books and appeals dealing with current questions of belief, as well as with human rights and issues of religious freedom. He defended the Church from the slander meted out to it in the Soviet press, and called on the hierarchs to stand up to the authorities. These articles were widely circulated in *samizdat* and read by young people and the intelligentsia. In 1972 Igor Shafarevich, a corresponding member of the Academy of Sciences and a member of the Human Rights Committee headed by Academician Andrei Sakharov, presented a report to the Committee on Religious Legislation in the USSR. Vladimir Osipov, a Christian intellectual, tried to provide a forum for "loyal opposition" to the Government in the shape of the journal *Veche*, which was self-published and widely circulated. Contributors wrote as Christian citizens of the Soviet Union on a wide range of topics. *Veche* appeared between 1971 and 1974, then Osipov was arrested for "anti-Soviet propaganda" and sentenced to eight years' strict regime camp. Meanwhile small groups of Orthodox Christians had begun to hold informal meetings to exchange their views on religion and philosophical issues. One of these, in Moscow, was led by Alexander Ogorodnikov, a recently converted student. "The Christian Seminar on Problems of the Religious Renaissance", as it was called, held meetings in members' flats. From 1976 the Seminar was subjected to KGB harassment, and in November 1978 Ogorodnikov was arrested and sentenced under Article 70 to six years' strict regime labour camp, to be followed by five years' internal exile.

The seminar and groups like it have clearly performed a very useful and much needed function given the almost total lack of Christian literature and opportunities for education and fellowship in the USSR. The Seminar members were convinced that "our problems were being raised neither in Church sermons, which are the only means of religious education, nor in the pages of the *Journal of the Moscow Patriarchate*, which is of course inaccessible to ordinary Christians. Above all, in the Russian Orthodox Church the parish is not like a brotherly community where Christian love of one's neighbour becomes a reality. The State persecutes every manifestation of Church life, except the performance of a religious cult. Our thirst for spiritual communion, religious education and missionary service runs up against all the might of the State's repressive machine".[17]

In 1975 Father Gleb Yakunin and a physicist Lev Regelson wrote an appeal to the Fifth Assembly of the World Council of Churches meeting in Nairobi. They called on the Western Churches to return to the early tradition of honouring confessors of the faith and to defend religious freedom throughout the world. They also wrote an open letter to Dr Potter, the WCC Secretary-General pointing out the legal discrimination against religion in the USSR. Meanwhile in 1973 another Orthodox priest, Father Dimitri Dudko, a friend of Father Gleb Yakunin, began a series of question and answer sessions in his church after Saturday Vespers. These attracted large numbers of young people. Patriarch Pimen ordered him to stop, and in September 1974 he was moved to a country parish some fifty miles from Moscow. Yet people continued to travel out to listen to him, and he was dismissed in December 1975 in spite of appeals by his parishioners. In 1976 he was appointed second priest in the village of Grebnevo. Throughout 1979 he was continually harassed by the police, and was finally arrested by the KGB on 15 January 1980. After five months in prison he unexpectedly appeared on Soviet television and admitted "systematic fabrication and dissemination abroad of anti-Soviet materials". He also wrote a confession of his faults in a letter to the Patriarch. This both surprised and horrified his friends who had long supported him. However, shortly before his arrest Father Dudko wrote to a friend in the West: "It seems that 1980 will be a difficult year for us. Some have already been seized. Some congregations are shocked and horrified by the kind of priests arriving to take up duties in their churches. It is quite clear why the authorities put Father Yakunin away, they want to silence dissenting voices as far as possible".[18] This summed up the whole situation of the Church in Russia at the time.

Throughout the 1960s and 1970s Christian activists in the USSR attempted at various times to bring the difficulty of practising their faith to the attention of the West. The most determined effort of this kind came in the wake of the Helsinki Agreements of 1975 which the Soviet Union agreed to observe.

The "Christian Committee for the Defence of Believers' Rights in the USSR" was formed on 27 December 1976 by a number of Christians. Its aim was to "help believers to exercise their rights of living in accordance with their convictions". The founders and best known members of the Committee were Father Gleb Yakunin, Hierodeacon Varsonofi Khaibulin, and Victor Kapitanchuk, all members of the Russian Orthodox Church. Many other denominations which had been severely persecuted, such as Baptists, Pentecostalists and Seventh Day Adventists, had already formed their own bodies to try to protect their members' interests. The Committee did, however, concern itself with the rights of all believers, not just Orthodox. It was obvious to the Committee's founders that the leadership of the Church would do little to protect believers' legal rights, and so they declared that they would do this themselves. They described their aim as fivefold. First, to collect, study, and distribute information on the situation of religious believers in the USSR. Second, to give legal advice to believers where their civil rights were infringed. Third, to appeal to State institutions concerning the defence of believers' rights. Fourth, to conduct research, and as far as possible clarify the legal and factual position of religion in the USSR. And fifth, to assist in putting Soviet legislation into practice.

The Committee fulfilled the first and fourth aims by compiling and sending to the West 416 documents (2,819 pages) between its foundation in 1977 and 1980. The documents dealt with different things. Some dwelt on the situation of the Church. One was a detailed commentary on the new Soviet Constitution of 7 October 1977. Perhaps the most important was the "Report of Father Gleb Yakunin to the Christian Committee for the Defence of Believers' Rights in the USSR on the current situation of the Russian Orthodox Church, and the prospects for the religious revival in Russia".[19] This was dated 15 August 1979, and was an analysis of every aspect of life in the Church, providing information on how the Church was hemmed in and restricted by the State both by legislation and extra-legal actions of state officials, to the point where it virtually had no freedom left. However, Father Yakunin pointed out that in spite of this there was mounting interest in Orthodoxy, especially among young people. He said that the Moscow Patriarchate had not responded to this religious renaissance. And he made the proposal that Orthodox believers who found it impossible to practise their faith should follow the example of Protestants and Catholics within the USSR and operate outside the control of state bodies. He said that such unregistered Orthodox communities should at the same time acknowledge the Moscow Patriarchate and so remain in communion with the central historical Church. In this document he was not proposing schism, but an administrative device to counter state domination of the Church.

One updated "Appeal to Christians of the whole World" sent out by the Committee spoke of the need for Christian literature in the USSR. This appeal asked Christians to do all they could to provide books for Russia. Tourists were asked to help. "Let everyone who travels to Russia take with them at least one Bible and one Prayer Book, which are permitted to be taken through Soviet customs".[20]

Most of the Committee's documents were concerned with special cases of violations of believers' rights. They sought to achieve total accuracy and to provide many factual details and avoid sensationalism. Many of the documents record attempts by parishioners to have their churches reopened after the Khrushchev period. Their stories are ones of sad and futile pilgrimages around government offices, and of hard-won interviews with a series of indifferent and sometimes hostile officials. Few of the parishes mentioned succeeded in reopening for worship. Some parishes were plagued by morally dissolute priests. In Osh, Kirgizia, for example, the priest was a well-known drunkard and womaniser, and was kept in his position as parish priest by the local authorities in spite of continuous protests by the parishioners.

The Christian Committee documents thus convey information on the life of the Russian Orthodox Church which has helped Christians in the West to build up a picture of what was going on; a picture which would otherwise have been much less accurate and detailed.

Despite a clear statement by the Committee in its founding declaration that it had no political aims and was loyal to Soviet laws, the KGB soon began to take an interest in its activities. In April 1977 an article attacking Father Yakunin and three other Orthodox Christians appeared in the Soviet weekly *Literaturnaya Gazeta*. Such articles in the Soviet press are tantamount to an intent to arrest. It was in 1977 that a wave of arrests began, which overtook the Helsinki Monitoring Groups. On 16 December 1977 both Yakunin and Kapitanchuk were warned that they would be arrested if they did not abandon their activities. Yakunin was reported to have been offered freedom to emigrate abroad, but he declined. Further warnings followed together with house searches, interrogations, and finally arrest in November 1979. Father Yakunin was held for nine months' pre-trial investigation, and on 25 August 1980 was charged with "anti-Soviet agitation and propaganda" under Article 70 of the RSFSR Criminal Code. He was sentenced to five years' imprisonment to be followed by a further five years' internal exile. Since these arrests the Committee has considerably reduced its work, and the crackdown on all Russian religious activists during the summer of 1980 seems to have largely brought this movement to a close.

Open persecution of the Church ceased with Khrushchev's removal from the political scene, but pressure and discrimination of all kinds continued. The first CRA Statute in 1966 and the amendments to the Laws on Religious Associations in 1975 demonstrate the authorities' unabated hostility to religion. It took three main forms. First, it became far more difficult to open a house of prayer. In the past you applied to the local Soviet who had to reply within a month. Article 7 of the 1975 amendment said, however, that religious associations might not even submit an application to the local Soviet until the CRA had given permission to register. Now (1986) they do not have to reply within any set period and any right of appeal has been removed. Second, the CRA could decide to close a church, and could also remove individual members from the executive body of a religious association. Third, the amendment also specifically forbade any voluntary church collections to be taken outside a church building, and required "special permission from regional or city Soviets for services to be held outside and also in the homes of believers".[21] The net result of the amendments was to give more power to the CRA. On the other hand, there were some positive points for the churches. In as much as they were now allowed to buy "church utensils, cult objects, means of transport; to rent or construct buildings for their needs in accordance with established legal procedure", they have tacitly been accorded legal status. But although the Church could now buy property, the actual church buildings remain firmly the property of the State and as such can still be confiscated at any time.

The policy of the State for the past five years has been to

allow certain concessions to the Church in return for the latter's continuing loyalty. In 1980 a new large plant was opened at Solrino near Moscow for the production of candles, incense, and other church utensils, and in 1981 the Patriarchal publishing house was moved from the Novodevichy Monastery to a new building in Moscow. The Church has to pay the highest price for materials, however, because it is classed as a private enterprise. The press has continued to produce the *Journal of the Moscow Patriarchate* as well as a new edition of the Bible, a prayer book, a psalter and a priest's manual.

While allowing some concessions to the Church as an institution, the State has, however, continued to promote anti-religious propaganda and education, and to discourage widespread interest in religious practices. It is a well known fact, for example, that the churches are cordoned off at Easter by the authorities on the pretext of protecting them against anti-religious hooligans, but also to prevent young people from attending the services. Thus there continues to be a discrepancy between the claim that religious believers enjoy freedom to practise their faith and the fact that they are systematically discriminated against if they attempt to do so.

To sum up, there has been a considerable religious revival in Russia since the end of the Second World War. There was a religious revival in the immediate post-war period, when the Church was able to build up its strength after the destruction of the 1930s. It was this amazing return to life which provoked Khrushchev's renewed persecutions. Since Khrushchev's fall, thousands of young people who belong to the second and third generations of Soviet citizens, and who have been brought up with a totally atheistic education, have been converted to Christianity. The revival which began in Moscow and Leningrad at the end of the 1960s had by the 1970s spread outwards into the provinces and this is still happening. This latest revival demonstrates the continuing resistance of the people to an atheistic regime.

However, there is a difference between the believers of the immediate post-war period and those of today. The post-war Christians had something of a religious background inherited from before the Revolution. The young Christians of today, however, belong to a generation brought up long after the Revolution, and have had to discover faith for themselves. For them Marxism–Leninism is dead, and they want to return to Orthodoxy as the true expression of Russian religious culture. For this reason many young Russian Christians are extremely conservative and tend to idealise the pre-revolutionary past. This can be explained by the fact that Soviet schools have no religious teaching at all, and so there is a total ignorance of church history and the part played by the Church in Russian life before 1917. There is another difference too. The young Christians of today do not feel so constrained by the laws on religious associations. They know that the only way to deal with a restrictive regime is to operate outside the law. Therefore, they will gather in flats for Bible study, and make their views known in *samizdat*. In fact by the mid-1970s almost 50% of all *samizdat* was written by religious believers.

How do the authorities react to this increased interest in religion amongst young people? They admit that "school-children show a largely positive attitude towards religion", and that 80% of all religious families teach religion to their children. They are concerned too by the influence of foreign broadcasts, as well as by the influx of religious literature smuggled into the USSR. They know that as many as 50% of all babies are baptised, and that young people are drawn into the Church in times of trouble. Added to this they are aware of the increased interest in religion among the Russian intelligentsia. A recent source says that of the 460 students at the Leningrad Theological Seminary 75% are adult converts or reconverts to Orthodoxy, and many already hold Soviet secular higher education diplomas prior to their theological enrolment.[22]

Father Borovoi summed up the atmosphere in a sermon at London's Russian Orthodox Cathedral in 1979 when he said: "a new movement has begun amongst educated youth. This generation has gained its conversion to Christ on its own, by way of the most profound reflections and inner trials. They come to us in different ways . . . this often results in the break-up of families, educational and professional sacrifices, even the need to part with a loved one; a bride or a fiancé with whom you have to part because he or she took fright of your road. And now we have hundreds and thousands of such *living* examples . . . that is what is new in our Church . . . the Lord has tested the faith of the Russian people . . . in these 60 years we have had thousands of times more Saints than in the rest of the history of the Russian Church. So that today living Saints walk the face of the earth in Russia".[23]

Even as I write we hear of new repressive measures beginning in Russia. The arrest of the religious rock musician Valeri Barinov on 4 March 1984 shows that the authorities' attitude to belief has not fundamentally altered. They are forced to live with the fact that the Church survives and remains a force in Soviet society, but they want to restrict its activities as much as possible. The Government is in a difficult position. On the one hand it wants to convince the West that there is religious freedom in the USSR, in order, if nothing else, to improve the Soviet Union's international image. For this reason most of the open churches are to be found in the major cities visited by tourists. Yet on the other hand the Government feels the need to control the Church because it poses a potential ideological threat. It does this in the great variety of ways outlined in this book. It is symptomatic of the dual nature of the Church that while the hierarchs travel abroad purveying political propaganda and promoting Soviet foreign policy aims, no priest or believer within the Soviet Union may express a Christian view on any social or political matter. And finally, we in the West have to look below the surface of Russian life to understand what is really going on. Things are not always what they seem to be.

# 4

# A Background to Soviet Laws on Religion

What were the doctrinal reasons for the Soviet Government's anti-religious attitude and its suppression of the Churches in Russia?

Lenin took much of his thinking on religion from Marx, who said: "Man makes religion, religion does not make man".[1] Marx and Engels argued that religion emerged from material causes. Man was unable to control his environment or explain natural phenomena, so he was frightened. This fear caused our ancestors to deify those very forces they could not control. Marx argued that as society developed, a class system grew up and the ruling classes adopted religious ideology as a tool to maintain and strengthen social inequality. Thus both Marx and Engels regarded the struggle against religion as a part of the class struggle. As Marx said in his now famous quotation: "Religious suffering is at the same time the expression of real suffering and a protest against real suffering. Religion is the sigh of the oppressed creature, the heart of a heartless world, just as it is the spirit of spiritless conditions. It is the opium of the people".[2]

Lenin duly described religion as "a sort of spiritual booze, in which the slaves of capital drown their human image, their demand for a life more or less worthy of man".[3] In other words, Lenin's argument was that religion prevented working people from doing something about their condition and "willed them away from revolutionary action, undermining their revolutionary spirit and destroying their revolutionary determination".[4] In his view "the deepest root of religion today is the socially downtrodden condition of the working masses and their apparent complete helplessness in the face of the blind forces of capitalism, which every day and every hour inflict upon ordinary working people the most horrid sufferings and most savage torment, a thousand times more severe than those inflicted by events such as wars, earthquakes etc".[5] In the new Soviet State there should be freedom of religious belief as well as the right not to profess any religion. However, Lenin stressed that the Bolshevik Party as such was opposed to all religions. Although faith must be a private affair as far as the State was concerned, the Communist Party "cannot and must not be indifferent to lack of class consciousness, ignorance and obscurantism in the shape of religious beliefs".[6] The Party was thus committed to an anti-religious programme from the start.

Lenin saw that the Russian Orthodox Church possessed enormous amounts of property and duly branded it an exploiter of the toiling masses. "The churches and monasteries own 6 million dessiatines[7] of land", wrote Lenin.[8] Thus millions of peasants suffered from land hunger. Whereas on average there were 40 dessiatines of land per monk or nun, peasants had to survive with their whole families on far less.[9]

As we saw in Chapter 2 in the late Tsarist period the Russian Orthodox Church was a part of the state apparatus. The clergy were expected to support the *status quo* and to threaten punishments on earth and in the life to come for those who questioned it.

Immediately after taking power the Soviet Government issued the "Declaration of the Rights of the Peoples of Russia" of 2 November 1917. This abolished all national and religious privileges and restrictions. It did away with the pre-eminent position of the Russian Orthodox Church as the State Church of the Russian Empire, and equalised the legal status of all religious sects in the Soviet Union.[10] Towards the end of 1917 several legislative acts concerning religion were announced. On 11 December 1917 an ordinance was issued above Lenin's signature ordering all religious organisations to transfer their "schools, academies, lower, intermediate, and higher schools and institutions" to the People's Commissariat of Education. All land including that belonging to the church was to be nationalised. Finally, all state funds given for the upkeep of churches and clergy were to be stopped.

However, the first really comprehensive legal act concerning religious life was issued on 23 January 1918 in the form of a Decree of the Council of People's Commissars. It was entitled: "On Separation of Church from State and School from Church".[11]

The main provisions of the instruction were as follows: the property of all religious sects was to be turned over to the local Soviets of Workers and Peasants Deputies, an inventory of all properties had to be submitted, and the property could then be returned to the worshippers for their use free of charge, provided that a group of at least twenty persons would assume responsibility for the property and its upkeep. This was the first time that the idea of the *dvadtsatka* or "group of twenty" as the basic unit of a religious association was introduced. It is still in use today, but the group's functions and responsibilities have been elaborated in greater detail over the years. The *dvadtsatka* was charged with making all repairs and paying all expenses necessary to maintain the property. If no group of twenty was willing to take responsibility, the church was to be closed. As far as the right to build a new house of prayer was concerned, the procedure required that the responsible *dvadtsatka* deposit an unspecified sum of money in the state treasury as a guarantee that the building would be completed. In reality this provision left ultimate control in the hands of the authorities, since they could set the amount of money required.

Other restrictions were placed on religious activity. First, all religious instruction was to cease in state, public, or private educational institutions. It was to be restricted to seminaries. Second, all records of birth, marriages, and deaths, which had previously been kept by the Church, were to be turned over to the local Soviets. Third, public processions could be held only with the advance permission of the local authorities. And fourth, all religious services and religious objects like icons were banned from public buildings.

The local authorities began to implement the Decree of 23 January and in many areas did this with such zeal that on 3 January 1919 a circular was issued pointing out that mistakes were being made in the interpretation of the instruction. This "Circular on the Problem of the Separation of Church and State" said, for example, that a house of prayer was to be closed *only* if a *dvadtsatka* (group of twenty) could not be found to assume responsibility for it – or if the local Soviet, in order to satisfy a *genuine* need for suitable quarters for public use or the "demands of the working masses", should decide to close it. The implication as to what had been going on was clear. Great efforts were now made to ensure that local authorities did not overstep the mark. Ridicule and humiliation of clergy were to be avoided. Similarly, unseemly forced labour such as cleaning the streets was not to be given to clergymen. Such punishments would anger believers and cause them to regard the clergy as martyrs. Thus, the circular continued, religious prejudices and the obscurantism of superstition were not to be fought "with the aid of punishment, but with an improved educational system, propaganda of communism, and with the organisation of the economy on communist principles".[12]

The 23 January Decree and the instruction that followed it provided the essential framework for religion in the years of Soviet rule, but they failed to solve all the legal problems that subsequently arose. It was necessary to issue further decrees to clarify one or another problem. One example concerned the right to give religious instruction. The extent of this right remained unclear for many years and varied from republic to republic. The Commissariat of Public Education issued a circular on 3 March 1919 stating that "teaching religious doctrines to persons below the age of eighteen is not permissible".[13] This circular contradicted the decree of 23 January 1918, which had stated that religious subjects might be taught and studied in a private manner. Two years later on 23 April 1921 the Commissariat of Public Education issued an explanation in which it said that what it really meant was that "religious teaching outside religious institutions (i.e. seminaries) should not assume the form of regularly functioning educational institutions".[14] As late as 1924 yet another interpretation was given: persons below the age of eighteen could receive religious instruction only at home. "At home" might mean in the home of the child, or of a clergyman or other instructor. The instruction, however, should not be a regular class and the group could not include more than three children.[15] This ruling applied only in the RSFSR, the regulations in the Ukraine were stricter.

Together with the entire legal system, the decree of 23 January was reorganised in line with the new Constitution of 3 July 1918, and accepted by the Fifth Congress of Soviets on 10 July 1918. The Constitution adopted Communist doctrine as the basis of its provisions and as the framework for future legislation. As far as religion was concerned, it guaranteed religious freedom so long as it did not conflict with the law. In other words, it recognised "the right to religious and anti-religious propaganda" for all citizens.

The most important provisions of the July Constitution as regards religion were contained in Articles 13 and 65. The former recognised the decree of 23 January 1918, and thus gave Constitutional sanction to the destruction of religious institutions, together with their property, laws, customs, privileges, and traditions. Article 65 was concerned with the secularisation of the clergy. They were stripped of all rights as citizens – even that of participating in local or state elections – and denied the freedom to move out of their parishes. Thus as a result of this Article they were politically and socially outlawed, and economically ruined. The Constitution appeared at first sight to guarantee basic freedoms, including religious freedom, but in fact sanctioned the anti-religious activity of the Communist Party as the leading, and soon only, party in the State.

In spite of these laws and decrees the supression of religion was not without its difficulties. Lenin felt that it would be impolitic to go too fast in the destruction of religion. The end of the period of War Communism and the introduction of the New Economic Policy, which included a measure of capitalism, saw him urging caution. In 1922 the Party issued *The Party Workers Handbook*, in which Party members were reminded that "the present period is not at all opportune for the pressing of the anti-religious struggle".[16] In 1925 the Commissariat of Internal Affairs issued a circular on the question of religious ceremonies in the homes of believers. It stated that "the performance of religious ceremonies within the homes of believers, like that of religious ceremonies in church, is permitted without hindrance or special permission".[17] This was reiterated in later legislation and was apparently still in force until 1975, although in practice it had not often been respected.

As the 1920s drew to a close, the regime felt that it was strong enough to enact new laws. Lenin was dead and Stalin had succeeded him. The Five-Year Plans, designed by Stalin to achieve a pure socialist economy, replaced the NEP (New Economic Policy). In the area of religion the often ambiguous policies of the 1920s were replaced by more forceful and aggressive measures. On 8 April 1929 a Standing Committee on the Affairs of the Cults was established, which was attached to the Presidium of the All-Union Central Executive Committee. On 8 April the "Decree on Religious Associations" was also issued;[18] and on 1 October 1929 the "Instructions of the People's Commissariat of the Interior" subtitled "On the Rights and

Obligations of Religious Associations" appeared, clarifying
and supplementing the April law.[19] These two documents
suggested that the regime believed the 1918 laws had not
fully provided for many aspects of religious activity, leaving believers too much room for manoeuvre, and that
more comprehensive and more detailed directives were
necessary.

These two acts of 1929 remain in force today, and for this
reason it is necessary to discuss them at length. To simplify
matters I shall do this theme by theme.

1. Members of a sect, denomination, or doctrine who are
eighteen years old and over may form "religious associations" or "groups of believers". Members may perform
religious rites, arrange prayer or general meetings of
believers, and manage religious property. The law then
enumerates activities not allowed to these associations or
groups, and in so doing restricts them to the performance of
purely religious rites and ceremonies. For example, it is
illegal to give material aid to other members of a religious
organisation, to establish libraries, reading rooms, or dor-
mitories for the poor. In exchange, religious societies are
allowed to receive free of charge, under contract from the
local Soviet, prayer buildings and objects used for worship
(icons, chalices etc). Under this law the clergyman has to
live in the area where his house of prayer and congregation
is located.

The law in fact makes provision for two types of religious
organisation: the "religious association", in other words
the *dvadtsatka* or group of twenty, and the "group of
believers", which may number less than twenty. The
specific legal status of the latter is unclear, but there is
ample evidence that the right to establish a group of
believers has seldom been granted. In other words, it is
important to realise that the only religious group recognised in practice is the *dvadtsatka*, the group of twenty. In a
"Summary of Information Relating to the USSR", submitted to the United Nations by the Soviet Government in

1959, the portion dealing with conditions under which religious associations may be formed says nothing about groups of less than twenty members.[20]

Any member of the *dvadtsatka* may withdraw at any time. If that were to happen the number of responsible members would be less than twenty and the contract of lease would be liable to be annulled. Should new members volunteer to replace those who have withdrawn, registration must be gone through all over again and a new contract drawn up. Again, it is very easy for the authorities to harass members of the *dvadtsatka*: all they have to do is remove a person's job or change his area of residence. Other pressures may be put on the *dvadtsatka* such as the invocation of paragraph 29d. This law imposes on the signing members the responsibility of paying the State for any damage done to the house of prayer. There is the threat of exorbitant costs for real or imagined damage. The law is known to have been effective in getting members to withdraw from the twenty, and so enable the authorities to close the church. If this fails, the authorities can invoke paragraph 14, which gives them a right to remove individual members from the executive board of an association. In all these ways the law and instruction of 1929 are not just legislative acts, but signify a much harsher environment for religion. The devastation that accompanied them in the 1930s has already been discussed in Chapter 2.

2. Every religious group has to be registered along with a list of its founders. The registration agencies must register the group within a month or inform it that registration is refused. Paragraph 46 of the instruction says that registration must be refused "if the religious association's methods and forms of activity are contrary to the laws and in effect threaten public order and safety, or provoke discord or hostilities among the nations". It is very easy, then, for the authorities to deny registration in the first place, and if they do grant it to keep a close eye on all members of the group.

3. Members of a religious society are allowed to make collections inside the church building. Donations may only be taken outside the building from members of the religious association, unless special permission is granted. No compulsory membership fee may be taken. The funds collected may be spent only in connection with the religious property on the performance of rites, and on remuneration of the clergy, singers, and watchman. All religious property must feature in an inventory to be kept with the civil authorities. Thus everything in the church belongs to the State, and in effect becomes a part of the lease agreement.

4. A religious society has to elect an executive body of three members. The registration agencies have the right to remove any individual member from the executive body.

5. Prayer meetings taking place in buildings made for that purpose (i.e. churches) which are considered satisfactory from a technical and sanitary point of view, may be arranged without notification to or permission from the authorities. Prayer meetings held in buildings not designed for that purpose (i.e. private houses or flats) may be arranged but only with permission for each separate meeting. A religious society must notify the authorities in advance of a series of prayer meetings to be held within a period of no more than one year. But at the same time the law is ambiguous. For paragraph 22 states that "believers who have not formed a society or group must notify the authorities regarding each separate prayer meeting". This implies the right of a non-registered group to exist and to hold religious ceremonies, such as prayers, requiem masses, baptisms, the bringing in of icons and the like, "in the home of believers without notification to or permission from the authorities", and there appear to be no specific restrictions on the numbers allowed to take part in such rites. Yet despite this provision prayer meetings in homes have been subject to disciplinary action and so are usually held clandestinely. It is fair to say that after various

"test cases" on this point the Commissariat of Justice declared that citizens may conduct prayer meetings in their own homes, provided they have submitted information on the time and place of such meetings to the authorities.

Special permission must be sought for general assemblies of religious societies, such as Church Synods. The local Council for Religious Affairs of the Council of Ministers may give permission, unless such a meeting "conflicts with the law and threatens social order and safety or provokes discord and hostility among the nations".

6. No religious rites, ceremonies or displays of cult objects are allowed in public institutions, with the exception of rites for those who are dangerously ill in isolated rooms in hospital, or burials in cemeteries and crematoria. However, permission is not required for religious processions around the prayer building if they are part of the religious service; otherwise permission is required.

7. A Religious Association has to submit a list of all its members according to established form. By 1 January each year any changes in that list must be entered, and if this is not done the registration agency may remove the members of the executive body and elect new ones.

8. The activities of Religious Associations are subject to surveillance by the CRA. It, as well as authorities whose duty is to "safeguard the revolutionary order and safety", may send their representatives to each assembly or meeting for the purpose of "watching over order and safety". Routine inspection of religious societies may be carried out at any time by the CRA.

9. If a Religious Association does not keep the rules the registration agency shall demand reform. If that does not happen, the City District Council for Religious Affairs may ask the Council for Religious Affairs of the Council of Ministers to liquidate the Association. An appeal against

this can be made within two weeks from the date of delivery of the decision.

In concluding this section on the 1929 legislation, we must remind ourselves again that the Constitution of the Russian Republic of 1924 contains a provision (Article 4) stating that "freedom of religious and anti-religious propaganda is recognised for all citizens". This accepted and enshrined the same point made in the 1918 Constitution (Article 13). Similar provisions had been made in the constitutions of the other Republics. But in May 1929 the 14th Congress of Soviets amended this provision, and the wording was changed to "freedom of worship and freedom of anti-religious propaganda are recognised for all citizens". In 1936 this new text became Article 124 of the "Stalin Constitution".[21] The use of the word "freedom" was meant to create the impression that the State was neutral on the question of religion. Of course, this was not the case because freedom for anti-religious propaganda was sanctioned but religious propaganda was illegal. This sums up the fundamental situation of religious associations in the Soviet Union. The Government gives atheists freedom of action and a legally recognised privileged position.

The situation of the Russian Orthodox Church radically changed from 1941, as a direct result of Hitler's invasion of the Soviet Union; yet even then the Church was never recognised legally as an institution: although in fact treated as such, the laws of 1929 were still in force. It should be remembered that throughout the period of Stalinist accommodation, anti-religious education and propaganda continued unabated.

After Stalin's death and the emergence of Khrushchev as Party Leader government policy towards believers radically changed. Khrushchev wanted to "normalise" relations between the secular authorities and the churches which in his view had been distorted since the War. He underlined the fact that the 1929 Legislation on Religious Associations was still in force. The 22nd Party Congress in

1960 adopted a resolution "On Tasks of Party Propaganda in Present-day Conditions" in which officials were reproved for taking a "passive, defensive position towards idealistic religious ideology, which is hostile to Marxism–Leninism". A further resolution reiterated the need to "educate people in the spirit of a scientific-materialistic worldview".[22] Khrushchev wanted Soviet education to free people from religious prejudices and superstition, and he called for an all-out effort to put this into effect among young people.

The 1929 legislation had remained unaltered for forty-four years, in spite of radical changes in government attitude throughout the period. But in July 1975 revisions were made which show a general tightening up of the existing system. It is thought that many of these new laws had already been in force since 1962, but had been kept secret. In a report since published in the West and presented to The Sakharov Human Rights Committee in May 1971, the Soviet mathematician Igor Shafarevich cited a recently published collection of legal documents. According to these changes had been made to the 1929 law by an Ukaz (decree) of the RSFSR Supreme Soviet on 19 October 1962, but these changes had not been made public.[23] This document is useful because it tells of unofficial State pronouncements up to 1971, and informs us of hitherto unknown laws which affect believers. Through it we can detect changing Government attitudes towards religion.

Much of the Ukaz was written into the new laws of 1975, so why was there the need for secrecy? The fact is that there is always a proportion of Soviet legislation that is never published. Shafarevich estimates that more than 80% of all "decrees" are not published.[24] Instead they are released to a limited number of agencies which will pass them on to subordinates in the form of administrative orders.[25] The Supreme Soviet passed a regulatory act in 1958 which stated (Article 3) that laws and decrees "not having general significance or not being of a normative character" need not be published, and only those persons affected need be informed. This should not apply to religious decrees, since in practice these affect a third of the population. The plain truth is that believers are made accountable for laws without always knowing their content.

Three main amendments to the 1929 legislation were published in 1975. Their implications can be summarised as follows.

1. Much more power has been placed in the hands of the CRA, who had previously served as an intermediary between Church and Government. This has removed authority from the local Soviet. In the 1929 legislation it was easier for a religious association to appeal against a decision made at the central office of the CRA, which was both geographically and hierarchically remote in Moscow. Moreover, in 1929 a decision for registration had to be made by the local Soviet, who had to reply within one month. The 1975 amendment said that registration had to be made through the CRA, who did not have to give a decision within any set period of time. On the one hand this move towards centralisation weakened the position of individual churches, but on the other hand it could make the Soviet Government more sensitive to foreign pressure over such things as the oppression of believers and closure of churches.

2. The amendments gave the Church the right to buy and own Church plate and other objects needed for worship, as well as to buy transport. It was also allowed to rent, build, and purchase buildings. These were small but welcome concessions.

3. The 1975 amendments in no way modified the legal position of the Church within the State. The Church is still not recognised as an institution in law. Certainly believers enjoy greater rights of possession through the *dvadtsatka*, the bishop, and the individual position of the Patriarch, but

these do not add up to an organisation or institution in the eyes of Soviet law. The latter is something that the Church has long fought to achieve. The situation is such that a prayer house may simply be closed by decision of the CRA, should it be needed for State or public purposes.

To sum up, then, the 1975 revision of the law on Religious Associations reflects a hardening of government attitudes towards believers, although these amendments have actually been in operation since 1962. The fact that they are now published in the Soviet Union is a step in the right direction, but many worrying features persist. For example, the wide discretionary powers of the CRA and continued disregard by the police of the laws on Religious Associations, lead to abuse. Under such conditions it is amazingly difficult for a believer to remain both a good Soviet citizen and a devout believer. Above all, the Soviet State does not live up to its guarantees of religious freedom set out in the Constitution and decree of 23 January 1918.

# 5

# Application of the Laws

Let us now look at how the laws operate in practice. Every year in the USSR many hundreds of religious believers are arrested, but only a relatively small proportion prosecuted. Some are released after investigation, many others are dealt with administratively and given sentences of up to fifteen days or fined. At this stage the offence is treated rather in the same way as a minor traffic incident in this country. On the whole it is the persistent offender who is arrested and sentenced. In any case, as pointed out in the last chapter, Soviet law is imprecise and there are still secret instructions unknown to citizens in the USSR that can be used to detain or arrest people.

However, essentially two groups of laws are used to arrest religious believers: those referring specifically to religious activity (Articles 142 and 227 of the RSFSR Criminal Code); and those dealing with, political or civil crimes (Articles 70, 190:1, 206, and 209 of the RSFSR Criminal Code).

Article 142 refers directly to violation of laws on the Separation of Church from State and School from Church. The first offence is punishable by "corrective tasks for a period not exceeding one year or by a fine not exceeding fifty roubles". Anyone committing the same offence for a second time is liable to "deprivation of freedom" for up to three years. Under Article 142 it is an offence to organise any activity in an unregistered church, or to teach religion to children other than one's own.

Article 227 says that it is an offence to organise or lead "a group whose activity, carried out under the guise of preaching religious doctrines and performing religious rituals, is connected with causing harm to citizens' health or with other infringements of the person or rights of citizens, or with inciting citizens to refuse to perform social activities or to fulfil civic obligations, and likewise enticing minors into such a group". This offence is punishable by deprivation of freedom for a period not exceeding five years or exile for the same period, with or without confiscation of property. In the Ukraine by a twist of penal law the equivalent Article 209 can carry a sentence of five years' imprisonment *followed* by five years' exile. Article 227, introduced in 1959, is directed particularly at Baptists and Pentecostals. The essential features are "causing harm to health", which is said to result from speaking with tongues, and "inciting citizens to refuse to do social activity", for example secular cultural activities. In practice this Article can be applied to almost any religious group, since both circumcision and baptism by immersion have been legally construed as harmful to health. In theory too the refusal to take part in atheistic activities such as courses of instruction in schools can be interpreted as refusing to participate in civic activities. Other examples of what constitutes doing harm to the health of citizens are such things as long fasts, or refusing to accept medical help.[1]

The Russian Orthodox Church suffers less from these Articles than the Baptists. The Orthodox remains the most "acceptable" Church to the Soviet Government, as its worship remains "conservative". The Baptists proselytise, widely ignoring government prohibitions. They have organised prayer meetings on religious holidays in the major cities of Rostov and Odessa. Reports say that thousands of believers have come from all over the country to attend these. At such meetings new converts are baptised, filling Baptist communities faster than they are emptied by arrests. The Orthodox priest Father Gleb Yakunin attributes the success of the Baptist missionary work to the fact that side by side with the registered communities there exists a semi-legal independent Baptist Church which refuses to register or to participate in other forms of government control. The official and unofficial churches are thus interdependent in the manner of interconnecting vessels. When the official Church is under pressure members transfer to the unofficial independent Church. The government hesitates to apply excessive pressure to the registered communities. Yakunin considers this to be the ideal structure for a Church under Soviet rule, because it enables it to sustain the heavy repressions inflicted by an aggressively atheistic government.[2]

The relative freedom of the registered Baptists is possible only at the expense of the independent Church, which has been persecuted for twenty years and particularly severely since 1980. The leaders of the independent Council of Churches, G. Kryuchkov, Nikolai Baturin and G. Vins were arrested in May 1966, and received three-year terms in labour camps.[3] Since that time all the members of the Council of Churches have been in hiding to avoid arrest. Most have served out several prison terms and constantly hide lest they be arrested again. Since 1971 the President of the Council, G. Kryuchkov, has lived successfully in hiding despite a countrywide search for him. In May 1974 a listening device was discovered in the electricity meter of his wife's apartment.[4] By 1981 almost all of the members of the Council of Churches with the exception of Kryuchkov had been imprisoned. They were all charged under Articles 142 and 227 of the RSFSR Criminal Code. The sentences were up to five years in strict regime camp, sometimes with internal exile afterwards.[5]

Baptist communities that refuse to register cannot have their own church buildings, yet services in private houses are prohibited. Such meetings are broken up by the militia and volunteer police, often in an extremely rough manner with insults and beatings. Ministers and community leaders are subject to arrest for holding prayer meetings outside a church, and are tried for violations of Articles 142 and 227 of the Criminal Code. If a minister does not work in a secular job but is provided for by the community, he can be charged with "parasitism" (Article 209 of the RSFSR Criminal Code) and sentenced to up to three years in camp. The host in whose house the service took place is also arrested and often charged with "hooliganism" (Article 206 of the RSFSR Criminal Code). He too can get from one to two years in strict regime camp.

Three examples of individuals arrested under these laws are especially interesting. The first is Ivan Fedotov, who at the age of fifty-six has spent over eighteen years in labour camps. He and his wife Valentina were told by the camp authorities that he would not get out alive. They have, however, been proved wrong. Fedotov suffers from bronchitis and heart trouble, and when his wife asked about his health at the camp in Arctic Russia where he was held the camp Commandant replied: "don't worry: if he dies, we'll put a cross on his grave". She knew the reality behind this threat, because she herself served a term of imprisonment for her activities as a Christian before she married Fedotov in 1971.

Ivan Fedotov grew up as a model Soviet citizen, serving in the navy for five years and taking a leading role in the Communist Youth League. However, in 1957 he became a Christian and joined a Pentecostal group. His leadership of the growing congregation led to his arrest on trumped-up charges of incitement to murder, for which he served ten years in prison. During this sentence he spent several periods in the punishment cells for possessing a New Testament and for converting other prisoners. After his release, and in the hope of avoiding further trouble, he joined a registered Baptist Church, but was expelled when some members became Pentecostals. He was arrested again in 1974 and sentenced to three years, then re-arrested in 1981 when he was sentenced to his current term of five years for "infringement of the person and the rights of citizens under the guise of performing religious rituals'', i.e. Article 227.

During his latest imprisonment Fedotov has been constantly victimised. On 22 September 1984 he was deliberately hindered from going to the bathhouse with his section of prisoners and had to go with another section; for this "violation of camp regulations" he was deprived of the next visit from his wife. He was then searched and five roubles were "found" in his boot. It is forbidden for prisoners to carry cash, so although Fedotov insisted that the money had been planted he was deprived of the right to use the camp shop and of his annual parcel due in October. He began a protest fast, for which he was sentenced to eleven days in the punishment cell. While there he committed another "violation" by allegedly failing to wash the floor properly, for which he was deprived of the next visit from his wife. He was then placed in the camp prison for three consecutive months as an additional punishment. Over the past three years he has been moved from two camps because of the number of prisoners who became Christians through his influence. In fact these repeated "violations" gave rise to fears that Fedotov's sentence might be extended under charges of "malicious disobedience to the camp authorities".[6] But fortunately these fears have proved groundless, and Fedotov was released on 21 April 1986.

Vladimir Murashkin was chosen to be pastor of the Maloyaroslavets Pentecostal Church when Ivan Fedotov was arrested in 1974. When Fedotov returned from prison camp the two worked together. Murashkin was born in 1944 and in August 1967 enrolled as a student at the Moscow Higher College of Decorative Industry. He became the union organiser and head student of his year group. But in 1969 after many years of searching for the truth he accepted the Evangelical Christian Faith and along with ten other students from the college joined the Moscow Church of Evangelical Pentecostal Christians. The authorities regard this church as illegal and are still persecuting it.

In the autumn of 1971 Murashkin was summoned to the Leningrad district KGB department and asked why he had accepted the Christian faith. He replied that he had been seeking the truth and had found it only in Christ, and so had given up his previous life-style of impurity, lying, and sexual promiscuity. The inspector tried to prove that sexual promiscuity is not a sin, but that combining religious faith with study at the institute is double dealing; if he did not give up his religious faith, Murashkin was told, he would not finish his course there. However, he refused to be swayed away from his new-found faith, and on 20 December 1971 at the end of his fifth term at the institute he and some of his Christian friends were dismissed for alleged unsatisfactory progress. Murashkin then became a painter employed by the Maloyaroslavets construction authority, as well as pastor to the Pentecostal Church.

Over the next years his and other believers' homes were searched. They were attacked in the press, fined, and the names of those attending services recorded. Finally in April 1981 both Murashkin and Fedotov were arrested at work. Their trial was held on 28 July 1981. Although officially only a few close relatives were allowed to enter the courtroom, Murashkin's wife was present in spite of the fact that she had been refused leave from work and threatened with dismissal if she went. Believers who had arrived to support their leaders spent the whole day outside the courtroom praying. Fedotov and Murashkin conducted their own defence. Murashkin was sentenced to five years' ordinary regime labour camp and confiscation of property under Article 227 of the RSFSR Criminal Code. He has been subjected to additional punishments during his time in labour camp. At the end of 1982 he was deprived of a visit from his family for alleged "violation of camp discipline".[7] Murashkin was released at the same time as Fedotov on 21 April 1986.

The third example of believers arrested under Articles dealing specifically with religion concerns two sisters. On 24 August 1983 Anna Shvetsova was arrested and sentenced to three and a half years ordinary regime camp under Articles 142:2 and 227:1 for running a Sunday School. She was twenty-one years old. Her twenty-two-year-old sister was charged with the same offence and sentenced to four years' ordinary regime camp. Both sentences were subsequently reduced by a year and the women transferred to a penal settlement. Anna Shvetsova completed her sentence in February 1986.

Let us now look at Articles of the criminal code which are not directly to do with religion but are nonetheless used to charge believers.

An increasing number of believers of all sorts are now charged under Article 70 of the RSFSR Criminal Code for "anti-Soviet agitation and propaganda". Under Anglo–American law criticism of government and state is reckoned to stand at the very heart of the democratic process. The Soviet Constitution of 1977 qualifies the rights of free speech, assembly and press by requiring that these must be exercised "in accordance with the interests of working people" and "with a view to strengthening the socialist system". Violation of Article 70 by writers and others is classified as an especially dangerous crime against the State. It can be committed by conversation, writing, speeches, and the displaying of flags. "Anti-Soviet" literature may take the form of books, pamphlets, articles, records, photographs, tapes and of course *samizdat*.

Punishment for first offenders is "deprivation of liberty for a period of six months to seven years, with or without additional exile for a period of two to five years; or exile for a period of five years". Subsequent violations are punishable by "deprivation of freedom for a period of three to ten years, with or without additional exile for a period of two to five years".[8]

Article 70 is capable of broad interpretation by the authorities and it is relatively easy for them to apply it to anyone who diverges from the party line. There are also some new changes in Article 70 which I shall deal with later in this chapter. In Chapter 3 I referred to the arrest of Father Gleb Yakunin and I now want to give other examples of those arrested under this law. Each shows in a different way the difficult position of believers in the USSR and how they can be arrested under this Article of the Criminal Code.

Tengiz Gudava, 31, and his brother Eduard are members of the Georgian unofficial musical ensemble "Phantom". Both brothers, their mother, and Tengiz's wife Marina have been under pressure from the KGB since 1978 for their religious and humanitarian activities. On 30 June 1985, Tengiz Gudava and another member of the "Phantom" group, Emmanuel Tvaladve, were arrested. Prior to arrest they were threatened with charges of treason, which can carry the death penalty in the USSR. The following account written by Tengiz Gudava shows what it is like to be charged, and what thoughts go through the victim's mind:

> The crime with which I am charged is considered to be serious, and the formulation of the charge is so monstrously absurd that I feel like a boxer reeling from a knock-out blow.
> They have now placed a gun at my head and say: your ideas, thoughts, feelings and convictions are "anti-Soviet agitation and propaganda", they "undermine" and "weaken" the Soviet government. What can I say in reply? Should I say "yes"? Should I say "no"?
> I can do neither . . . I wrote and said what I thought, felt, experienced. Maybe I am at fault by not having an internal "censor" in my brain which would stifle thought at its very conception? Or does my fault lie in that I am repelled by the nondescript, the monotonous, the grim?
> I am charged with my *samizdat* brochure *On The Primacy of Matter and its End Results*. I will only say that one of the main reasons behind the writing of this brochure was the desire to

clarify to myself in the first instance, the stance which a believer should adopt in a society that rejects God, for this is how I perceive a society based on Marxism-Leninism. I believe this question is one of vital importance for sincere believers and all honest citizens alike.

Yes, this question is a complex one, perhaps one of the most complex in the history of humanity. Yet it is one that must be faced by everyone who steps across the threshold of a church, who has suddenly perceived the radiance of being one of God's children, who wishes to witness Christ in word and deed, everywhere and always. I wrote my thoughts on this matter, without trying to impose my views on anyone.

The nature of the Soviet government's reaction is more an indictment than a thousand books or brochures such as mine. It is a classic illustration of the basic thesis outlined in my work: it is as impossible to avoid confrontation between belief in God and a godless regime as it is to combine ice and fire. In this I see the cross which is borne by every Christian living in an atheist empire. Christians in the West have their problems too, but here it is the first problem we encounter.

I have been in prison and labour camp, so I know what to expect. I do not want to rot within their walls, while the years, youth and life slide by never to return. I hate imprisonment, barbed wire, handcuffs, guards, desecration of human souls and bodies, violation of human dignity and deprivation of all meaning of life! I am 31 years old. The last seven of these years could hardly be termed "normal existence". I am tired. Like everyone I yearn for simple, human joys, work, a family, peace. The thought of twelve years imprisonment fills me with dread.

But there is no other way. My soul, the very essence of me, is to be placed on trial. To deny that of which I am accused would be to deny myself.[9]

My second example is Russian Orthodox Christian Natalya Lazareva, who was born in Leningrad in 1947. Her mother suffered from continuous ill-health as a result of injuries sustained during the shelling of Leningrad by the Germans, and Natalya spent long periods in a state-run children's home while her mother was hospitalised. Although she had obvious artistic gifts she was given no chance to develop these but was sent to work in a factory. While there Natalya managed to complete a "school for young workers" and enrol in the Institute of Theatre, Music and Cinematography, from which she graduated as an artist–producer. However, her diploma did not result in a job in Leningrad, and she was unable to look for work elsewhere because she had to look after her sick mother. Thus she became one of the Soviet Union's jobless, with no unemployment benefits, no right to ask for any assistance from the State, and under permanent threat of arrest as a "parasite" for being without work. She finally got a job as an instructor to a children's artistic circle, but this group soon dissolved for lack of funds. The next job she found was as a stoker at a gas works. The work was extremely heavy and totally unsuitable, but was made tolerable by the fact that her colleagues were the poet Oleg Okhapkin, the philosopher and literary critic Yevgeni Pazukhim, and several artists who were given no opportunity to exhibit because of their refusal to conform to the compulsory "socialist realism" style of painting. They too had been forced to take manual jobs despite their academic qualifications.

In March 1980 Natalya Lazareva was one of eight women who founded the first independent Christian Women's group in the Soviet Union – the "Maria" Club. Most of the founders were eventually forced to leave the USSR. In September 1980 Natalya was arrested and charged under Articles 190:1 and 196 of the RSFSR Criminal Code. During her trial she conducted herself with calm and courage. When the judge demanded to know why Lazareva asserted that the lot of women in the Soviet Union was an exceptionally hard one (contrary to all claims in the Soviet press), she replied simply: "Because I cannot say black is white". She was sentenced to ten months' labour camp. Her period in camp, among women forced to do heavy labour and suffering from constant hunger, was marked by a great deal of truly Christian selfless activity. She wrote letters and protests against unjust treatment and sentences for women who could not do this for themselves, and gave them moral support and shared her meagre rations with them.

On completion of her sentence Lazareva returned to Leningrad where, after first having been refused permission, she was eventually allowed to live for one year only – until October 1982. On 13 March 1982, however, she was arrested again and this time charged under Article 70 of the RSFSR Criminal Code, "anti-Soviet agitation and propaganda". Items confiscated from her home for presentation as evidence against her included articles for the journal of the "Maria" club and a copy of the first issue of this journal to be published in the West by the "Maria" club members expelled from the USSR.

Lazareva was put under pressure to collaborate with the KGB investigation of the group, and was allowed to telephone her friends from prison to tell them not to take any action in her defence, explaining that this could result in her getting a longer sentence. In March 1985 Natalya Lazareva was reported to be suffering from heart spasms, inflammation of the gall bladder and intestine, and high blood pressure.[10] Her four-year sentence to strict regime labour camp finished on 13 March 1986, and she has been relieved of her two years of internal exile. She is reported to have returned to Leningrad, but has not yet had official permission to live there.[11]

Article 70 is applied in cases where fundamental criticism has been made, for example of the USSR's record on human rights, or the treatment of national minorities. Another Article frequently used to charge believers is Article 190:1 of the RSFSR Criminal Code. "Circulation of deliberately false concoctions, slandering the Soviet State and social order". This is punishable by "deprivation of freedom for a period not exceeding three years, or by corrective tasks for a period not exceeding one year, or by a fine not exceeding one hundred roubles". Article 190:1 is often applied to believers who have written or spoken about religious persecution or have been involved in the circulation of documents detailing violations of religious freedom and other human rights. Yet it is not in fact clear if there is any difference in the type of activity which may incur punishment under these two Articles. It seems fairly arbitrary which Article is used.

One of the best known examples of those charged under Article 190:1 is the case of Felix Svetov, whose wife Zoya Krakhmalnikova is herself serving five years' exile for editing the *samizdat* journal *Nadezhda* (Hope). Svetov was arrested on 22 January 1985 following a house search. Both Svetov and his wife had been members of the Soviet literary establishment before becoming active believers. In fact Svetov had incurred the wrath of the authorities in his autobiographical novel, *Open Doors for Me*, which describes his own conversion. He also defended the rights of writers under pressure from the State, namely Sinyavsky and Daniel as well as more recently Academician Sakharov. This cost Svetov membership of the prestigious Writers Union. He described Sakharov as "one of the most wonderful people of our time". It has been reported recently that Svetov's case has been taken over by the Procurator-General of the Soviet Union, Alexander Rekunkov. It is unusual for the Procurator-General to take personal charge of such a case. But it is also reported that Svetov, who suffers from asthma and a heart condition, has had to share a cell with sixty others for two months, most of whom smoked. As a result of this he has had to be hospitalised. Svetov was tried in Moscow on 8 January 1986 under Article 190:1, and according to the Tass report was sentenced to a period of "temporary banishment" from Moscow. In practice this means a five-year sentence which was reduced to three years. Recent reports confirm that he has arrived at Ust-Koksa, a village in the Gorno-Altai autonomous region of the RSFSR. He took a month to get there, and has recently had a visit from his wife who is serving a sentence in exile in Ust-Kan about 80 miles away.[12]

Another problem for believers is the publication and distribution of religious literature. The authorities try to prevent this under Article 162 of the RSFSR Criminal Code, "Engaging in a prohibited trade". The actual production of literature is not in itself illegal, but operating a private printing press is. Under this Article "if committed on a significant scale it [operating a private printing press] is punishable by deprivation of freedom for a period not exceeding four years with or without confiscation of property". There are regular reports of police searches of private homes in various parts of the Soviet Union, during which large quantities of unofficially produced literature are confiscated. During one search in October 1974 at a farm in Estonia the police confiscated 15,000 Bibles. Nine Baptists were arrested and all sentenced for "engaging in prohibited trade". After a similar police search in Ivangorod, a town in the Leningrad region, in March 1977 nine tons of paper, printing equipment and religious literature were confiscated and four Baptists were arrested. All were tried in November 1977 and given from three to five years' imprisonment.[13] In late 1984 30,000 printed Bibles and six tons of paper were seized when a secret Baptist printing press was discovered near Alma Ata in Kazakhstan.

Father Alexander Pivovarov's is another such case. He was arrested, and charged under Article 162, sentenced to three and a half years in a strict regime labour camp and his property was confiscated. He had served faithfully as a parish priest in the Siberian town of Tomsk, where he became known as an inspired preacher and was called "the light of Siberia". But he also attracted the attention of the KGB, who instituted a year-long investigation after which he was accused of "inciting fanaticism" in the masses by spreading delusions. He was then slandered in the Soviet press. In 1975 Pivovarov became secretary to Archbishop Gedeon in Novosibirsk. At the same time he helped distribute unofficially produced religious literature, much of which had not been seen for decades. As we have said, religious literature is in very short supply and so has to be produced unofficially to meet the demand. It was this activity that brought the final blow from the KGB. His house was searched in April 1982 and the KGB confiscated his Bible, prayer book and other religious materials, along with money and his typewriter. He was immediately dismissed from his post as secretary to the Archbishop and given no alternative work for six months. Then he was sent to the town of Yeniseysk, the northernmost parish in the diocese. His arrest came on 11 April 1983, and he was tried and sentenced for engaging in an illegal trade in Novosibirsk in the autumn of that year. In addition to the traumas of her husband's arrest, trial and imprisonment, Pivovarov's wife has had to watch whilst property was confiscated from their home.

Two further Articles used to detain believers are 206, "Hooliganism" and 209, "Parasitism". It is quite common for the authorities to imprison people under Article 206 when they want to remove them from circulation because of purely religious activities which are not readily punishable under any other Article. A charge of "hooliganism" can be built up on the flimsiest of pretexts. It is punishable with up to five years' imprisonment, or up to seven years' if any sort of weapon was involved. However, this Article is criticised by the judiciary for its imprecise definition. It refers to hooliganism as "intentional actions violating public order in a coarse manner and expressing clear disrespect towards society". One example of this is a peaceful demonstration for permission to emigrate from the USSR.

In some cases the authorities deliberately fabricate incidents to lend credibility to such charges. For example, Vadim Smogitel, a Ukrainian musician who applied to emigrate after being harassed by the authorities since the 1960s, was arrested and charged in December 1977 after an incident which was described as follows in the Moscow *samizdat* journal *A Chronicle of Current Events*:

> On 12 December 1977 Smogitel said in a telephone conversation to Canada, "get me out of here somehow". The next day, when Smogitel was walking alone down the street in the evening a man fell under his feet and immediately police and volunteer militia appeared at his side.

According to the indictment against him, Smogitel "attacked the man in the street and struck him, causing him to fall and receive serious injury". He was sentenced to three years' imprisonment.[14]

Article 209 of the RSFSR Criminal Code as amended in 1975 states that "parasitism" is: "systematically engaging in vagrancy or begging and also leading any other parasitic way of life over a protracted period of time". It is to be punished by "deprivation of freedom for a term of up to one year or by corrective labour for the same term. If committed by a person previously convicted under the first paragraph of this article, these acts shall be punished by deprivation of freedom for a term of up to two years". This Article has been further amended in 1983 to give maximum sentences of two and three years. Thus a "parasite" is a person who is fit for work and lives on "unearned income with avoidance of socially useful work for more than four months in succession or for periods adding up to one year". In these cases the local authorities will warn the person and give him one month in which to take employment. If the person does not respond to the warning he is warned again and given a second month, after which he is liable to prosecution. This law is especially dangerous for believers because they are often dismissed from their jobs for nonconformist behaviour. This applies to those in professional posts and ordinary workers, as well as to released prisoners of conscience who often have great difficulty in getting employment. In many cases dismissed scientists and other professional people have been unable to find even the most menial work, since the authorities may well put obstacles in the way of their finding work at all. The threat of "parasitism" hangs over people who seriously want to find work, or it is used as an initial means of arrest before a more serious charge can be brought under the Criminal Code.

Such is the case of Peter Peters, a youth evangelist and pastor of an unregistered reform Baptist church who was arrested for the fourth time on 28 January 1984. Peters has felt not only the personal hardship of imprisonment but also the sorrow of seeing other members of his family imprisoned for their religious convictions. His father, brother, and another relative were sentenced in December 1981 and are at present in labour camps. Indeed another of his relations was arrested as recently as May 1985. Peter Peters was born in 1942 and first arrested in 1967, when he was sentenced to two years imprisonment. On 5 November 1969 two KGB officers tried to persuade him to collaborate with them. He was promised continual freedom if he agreed and prison if he did not. He gave them an unequivocal refusal. Later the two men came to his flat while he was out and made it clear that if they had found him in they would have arrested him.

From 1970 therefore he was unable to live at home. He was eventually arrested in 1973 and sentenced to three years' strict regime camp under Article 209 for "parasitism". Reports say that he worked as a prison locksmith during this sentence. Peters served the three years and was released, and later went to Rostov-on-Don as pastor to a congregation there. On 26 August 1977 a peaceful meeting of believers was broken up violently by the militia and Peter Peters and others were detained. He was released, only to be arrested on 3 January 1978 and was charged under Article 190:3. The charges were related to Christian gatherings, but believers from Rostov denied that their gatherings were public disturbances: they had been forced to carry on their services in the woods because they had been barred from their usual meeting place.

Telegrams of protest were sent by believers to Brezhnev, Kosygin and the Procurator-General of the USSR, but Peters' trial was still a travesty of justice. Its date was kept secret even from his relatives, and the authorities went to great lengths to hinder defence work by the lawyer Peters' father had hired. Believers found out about the trial the day before and managed to locate the building, but were only allowed in after the trial had begun. In addition to the two and a half year sentence, Peters was put into a category of prisoners who have a "tendency to flee" and are forced to wear a red stripe on their uniform. Many feared that this could be used as a pretext to shoot him if he were in the area designated as being off limits, i.e. beyond the camp perimeter.

While in camp Peters wanted a Bible but was refused the right to have one, so he went on a protest fast from 28 August to 12 September 1978. Sometime in 1979 a New Testament and a piece of Christian literature were discovered in his possession in the camp, and he was put into a punishment cell and deprived of his scheduled visit from relatives. He suffered other discrimination against him in camp as well: he was not allowed to send or receive letters which contained passages of scripture or discussion of religious themes. His mother's letters were denied him because they were written in German (his parents are of German origin and like many of her generation of Soviet Germans his mother has only poor Russian) and the camp authorities claimed there was no camp censor to read them. His red stripe was removed, however.

On 3 July 1980 Peters completed his sentence and returned to Rostov. He was refused a residence permit there on the grounds that he had no accommodation. A month before his release his father, brother and brother-in-law had been arrested and were sentenced to five, three, and three and a half years in a labour camp respectively. He was called by the authorities "public enemy number one". Little was heard of him from then on, although he sent out a warning in November 1981 that the KGB was using a new tactic to trap believers – strangers were coming to the homes of believers asking for money, saying it was needed for Peter Peters or the "Khristianin" unofficial printing press, and asking for the addresses of other believers. A sermon by Peters reached the West in 1983. We do not know the exact details of his activities since then, but he was arrested for the fifth time on 26 January 1984 in Tbilisi. He was sentenced on 22 May 1984 under Articles 190:1, and 209 "parasitism", to three years' strict regime labour camp.[15]

Under Article 80 of the RSFSR Criminal Code evasion of the call-up to active military service is punishable by "deprivation of freedom for a period of one to three years". The obligation of Soviet citizens to do military service is laid down in the USSR Constitution 1977 and runs: "Defence of the Socialist Motherland is the sacred duty of every citizen of the USSR". The details of compulsory military service are laid down in a law passed by the USSR Supreme Soviet on 12 October 1967 entitled "On Universal Military Obligation". This specifies that male citizens over the age of eighteen are liable to military call-up for a term of active service varying from one to three years according to the branch of the service and a man's educational qualifications. The only exceptions are people under criminal investigation or correction, those who are physically unfit, and those in full-time education. Any man can be called up until the age of twenty-seven.

This, of course, poses problems for religious pacifists and conscientious objectors, especially as everyone called up for service has to swear the military oath. This oath demands total commitment to the Soviet Union and can be at variance with their convictions. They swear: "to be loyal to my last breath to my people, my Soviet Motherland and the Soviet Government" and to "defend it courageously and capably, with dignity and honour, not sparing my blood or my life to win complete victory over the enemy". Religious conscientious objectors are continually pressured to renounce their convictions and take the oath.

Between June 1975 and May 1979 twenty-two Baptists, Pentecostals and Seventh Day Adventists are known to have been sentenced as conscientious objectors. The best documented case is that of Daniil Vashchenko, a Pentecostal from Nakhodka in the Maritime Territory in the Soviet Far East. Vashchenko was born in 1955, in May 1974 was called up for military service in Nakhodka, and on reporting was pronounced fit. He then stated orally and in writing that he would not bear arms or take the military oath because of his religious convictions. He offered to fulfil his military obligations by means of civilian labour without taking the military oath. But in Soviet law there is no alternative to purely "military" service and he was arrested under Article 80. At his trial in August 1974 his father argued that his son could not bear arms because of his pacifist views, that compulsory military service represents a restriction on "freedom of conscience" guaranteed by the USSR Constitution of 1936, and that in a 1919 decree Lenin had recognised the right of individuals to refuse military service on religious grounds. Vashchenko was sentenced to three years' imprisonment.[16]

The laws outlined here all stand today (1986), but recently there have been a number of changes that point to a further hardening of the system against believers. Most notably, on 11 January 1984 the Presidium of the USSR Supreme Soviet issued a decree introducing changes in the law of 25 December 1958 called "Criminal Liability for State Crimes". This new decree came into force on 1 February 1984, without waiting for the Supreme Soviets of the Republics to add amendments to the Criminal Code.

The most important change occurs in Article 7 of the law of 25 December 1958 (corresponding to Article 70 of the RSFSR Criminal Code and analogous Articles of the Union

Republics). The Article concerns "anti-Soviet agitation and propaganda". Part 2 of it, which lays down a penalty of up to ten years of camp and five years of exile, was formerly applied to people convicted more than once or as a result of activity carried out in war. Now, however, the same penalty is laid down for "activities carried out with the use of monies or other material goods, received from foreign organisations or persons acting in the interests of such organisations". No precise definition is given of "material goods". It would be easy to apply this to any kind of package or parcel. The law does not stipulate that "foreign organisations" should be "subversive" or "anti-Soviet", it is enough for them to be "foreign". Also "persons" giving aid do not have to be members of such organisations – it is enough for them to be "acting in the interests of such organisations". It follows that any humanitarian aid from any fund based anywhere abroad, or even from private individuals, may from now on be considered an aggravating circumstance in relation to criminal liability according to Article 70 of the RSFSR Criminal Code.[17]

The decree does not actually say that it is illegal to *receive* aid, but it is easy for the Soviet authorities to bring trumped-up charges against anyone on the basis of this clause should they wish to do so. In the past Soviet citizens have received aid reasonably openly. Cases are known of foreign currency being brought into the Soviet Union for the specific purpose of helping someone buy a flat. This sort of practice is now in considerable danger. Nevertheless, there is also evidence to show that aid of different sorts does get through, and that the new law has not had such a devastating effect as was at first feared. The fact remains that the new amendments to Article 70 can be used to cover something as trivial as receiving a pair of jeans, and any receipt of material aid from abroad can make matters worse if a citizen is charged under Article 70, "anti-Soviet agitation and propaganda".

Article 20 of the law (corresponding to Article 83 of the RSFSR Criminal Code, "illegal exit abroad", i.e. crossing the border), has been supplemented with a new clause. This makes repeated offences punishable not by up to three years' deprivation of liberty, but by five years'.

The best known examples of the application of this Article are the Christian rock musician Valeri Barinov, aged forty, and Sergei Timokhin, twenty-six. The two men were charged with attempting to cross the Soviet border illegally. Their trial at the Leningrad City Court lasted from 20 to 22 November 1984 and they were sentenced to two and a half and two years' ordinary regime labour camp respectively. The official Tass report of 23 November stated that: "it was established that they entered into criminal collusion in February 1984 and, with a view to crossing the border, arrived at one of the border stations in March". Tass claimed that "for several years they had maintained contacts with foreigners – representatives of anti-Soviet organisations abroad" and with the help of "emissaries of those organisations, Barinov and Timokhin had tried to smuggle slanderous information abroad on the position of believers in the USSR". Though the two were charged and sentenced under Article 83 of the RSFSR Criminal Code, it is clear from the Tass report that the real reason for their arrest was that they had "openly conducted religious propaganda".

Valeri Barinov is the leader of the rock group "Trumpet Call" and a composer of a Christian rock opera of the same name. He has in the past carried on evangelistic work using music as his medium, and he has built up wide support both inside the Soviet Union as well as abroad. After the arrest of the two men in March 1984, Barinov was first held in the Kresty Prison in Leningrad, then in a psychiatric hospital, and then in the KGB headquarters at Liteiny Bridge. While in Kresty Prison he conducted a twenty-two day hunger strike, and his health is reported to be weak as a result. Despite this Barinov went on another hunger strike demanding that the authorities allow him and his family to emigrate. He was force-fed in a brutal manner and suffered a heart attack. His appeal against his sentence was turned down, and he was sent to camp No. 27 in the Komi Autonomous Republic. The camp's population is made up of common criminals and is known by the grim nickname "blood-soaked 27". Beatings and killings are reported to be commonplace.[18]

A campaign for the release of Barinov gathered pace. Both David Steel and Neil Kinnock signed a joint appeal and addressed it to Mikhail Gorbachev. George Robertson, a labour MP who was in Moscow to mark the VE Day celebrations in May 1986, mentioned his case. The liberal MP, David Alton, tabled an Early Day Motion in the House of Commons which included this statement. "No evidence was produced at his trial to support the charges and his trial concentrated on the activities of his Christian rock group".[19] Barinov was released on 4 September 1986.

On 25 May 1984 the Chairman of the Presidium of the USSR Supreme Soviet, Konstantine Chernenko, signed a decree introducing new restrictions on contact between Soviet citizens and foreigners. The decree allows Soviet citizens to invite to the USSR on their personal initiative foreigners or persons without citizenship, to offer them lodging or convey them in a private car, only if they have permission from the local authorities. People who by the nature of their work have contact with foreigners, or work with documents concerning foreigners, are liable to a fine of 10 to 100 roubles for violation of the decree. Other citizens are liable to a fine of 10 to 50 roubles. This penalty is not very large, but it is significant that unrestricted association with foreigners should now be declared illegal. It clearly demonstrates the Government's worry that contact with foreigners might be detrimental to the Soviet system.[20]

This decree came into force on 1 July 1984. In the past there have been penalties imposed on Soviet citizens who have failed to register foreigners staying in their homes, but this new law makes contact even more difficult.

Arguably the most worrying of all is the new act of the Criminal Code No 188:3, which came into force on 1 October 1983. This gives administrative authorities in labour camps a new sanction against those who show "malicious disobedience" and have already been punished for breaches of camp discipline by a period of solitary confinement or prison. Such prisoners can now be punished by having a labour camp sentence extended by a period up to three years. "Especially dangerous state criminals" can be punished by an additional sentence of between one and five years. Into this category fall all those who are convicted under Article 70 of the RSFSR Criminal Code, "anti-Soviet agitation and propaganda."

This law means that anyone who is involved in a breach of camp discipline can now be kept in a labour camp, in effect, indefinitely. It will affect those who take part in hunger-strikes and other forms of protest, and indeed anyone who infringes any form of camp discipline down to such details as wearing an unbuttoned jacket, or lying on a bed during the daytime rest period. In other words this legal change makes it possible for many prisoners to have their sentences extended quite arbitrarily. It is virtually impossible for prisoners to go outside the camp without breaking some regulation or other, but the law is intended above all as a crackdown on the number of protests made by prisoners against conditions in camp.[21]

A particularly disturbing occurrence is the re-arrest of the Orthodox believer Vladimir Poresh, aged thirty-five, who was sentenced to a further three years' imprisonment in October 1984 under Article 188:3. Poresh was a junior researcher at the library of the Leningrad Academy of Sciences, and a founder member of the Christian Seminar. His arrest on 1 August 1979 aroused a wave of indignation. Protests came from members of the Christian Seminar as well as from a group of scholars who had been Poresh's former colleagues at the Academy of Sciences. Three of the latter addressed a statement of principle to the Leningrad

City Court, justifying their action on the grounds that "the civic conscience and duty of honest people do not allow us to keep silent and remain indifferent when we see the destinies of talented young men and women are being demolished before our very eyes".[22] Poresh was tried on 25 April 1980 and sentenced to five years' strict regime labour camp and three years' internal exile for "anti-Soviet agitation and propaganda."

This sentence was due to end on 1 August 1984. A day before his term was completed, however, a new criminal case was brought against him under Article 188:3. The trial was conducted at the famous Christopol Prison in the Tatar ASSR where he had been brought in 1982. Poresh was accused of not going to work and of disrespect towards the administration. According to a testimony given by a prison guard he had passed a note from one prison yard to another. As evidence the court produced a note in Hebrew, a language which Poresh does not understand. In fact Poresh and some others had refused to go to work for a period of two weeks in protest at an incident in which prison guards had broken the arm of a prisoner, Grigory-ants. The prisoners sent a complaint to the Procurator's office but received no reply. "When the Procurator's office failed to reply to the complaint and the appeals sent to him, the only form of struggle that remained to us was a strike", stated Poresh at his trial. His disrespect towards the authorities consisted in Poresh having written letters of complaint to the Procurator's office. One had been about the brutal beating of a prisoner in the cell next to his in the punishment area, and the other about the prison Governor's cutting down on the bread rations given to prisoners.

The trial lasted two and a half hours and concluded with a sentence of three years' deprivation of freedom in a strict regime labour camp, to be followed by the three years' exile.[23] Vladimir Poresh is married with three daughters, the youngest of whom was born after his arrest in 1979. Poresh's sentence was, however, unexpectedly quashed on 20 February 1986 after he had served only one and a half years of his three-year term. He has not been declared innocent of the charges, and remains under administrative surveillance. Although others have been sentenced under Article 188:3 subsequently, there may be grounds for hope that some will be similarly released.

A further example is Pastor Mikhail Khorev, a leader of the unregistered Baptist Council of Churches in the USSR. He completed a five-year sentence on 27 January 1985 and was sentenced the following day to a further two years' imprisonment. Khorev was re-arrested in camp on 22 November 1984, after money that had apparently been "planted" was found in his boot. He was transferred to an investigation prison. The possession of money in camp is a violation of camp regulations and Khorev, who has spent many periods in the punishment cells and camp prisons, was charged with "malicious disobedience towards the corrective labour institution authorities" under Article 188:3 of the RSFSR Criminal Code.

It is easy to see how useful this law is for controlling difficult prisoners who do not serve the interests of the regime.

Finally, there have been changes in Article 198:2 of the RSFSR Criminal Code, dealing with "malicious infringement of the rules of administrative surveillance". This "surveillance" refers to periods in which the prisoner will be under observation after completing his camp sentence. Until the latest changes came into effect on 1 October 1983, attempts to escape from places of exile or to evade surveillance could be punished by six months to a year in detention, and then only after two previous warnings within a year. The new law makes provision for detention of between one and three years for the first offender.[24]

All the evidence suggests that the recent changes in the law make it possible for sentences to be extended easily, and it remains to be seen how widely and how frequently the authorities will use their new powers. Indications are that the regime intends to be no less tough on dissidents of all sorts, including Christians of all denominations who are prepared to stand out for their faith. However, much of the foregoing evidence happened before the death of President Chernenko, and it will be interesting to see whether Mr Gorbachev will change direction. So far there has been little sign of this. Keston College reports on 22 August 1985 a continuing high wave of arrests of Soviet Baptists.[25] The Friedensstime Mission in West Germany reports the arrests of eleven more Baptists from the unregistered Baptist Churches. This continuing high number of arrests seems to dash any hopes of an early change of policy towards unregistered churches under the leadership of Mr Gorbachev.

# 6

# Harassment and Discrimination

We have talked at some length about arrest, and explained what happens under different laws. Yet many believers are considerably harassed by the authorities and discriminated against before they reach the point of arrest. This harassment is intended to warn people off religious activity and to cow believers into submission before they feel the full force of the laws. Many of the laws themselves, of course, act as a form of discrimination, in that believers are not able to practise their religion in a free and open manner and can only hold services in a properly registered building. The State owns and controls all existing places of worship, and a parish has no rights of legal redress for any injustice. Yet at the same time there is also severe discrimination in public life.

With a few exceptions, believers of all denominations are prevented from reaching positions of authority. Instances where believers have been expelled from the Communist Party, from managerial positions, or from teaching posts are common. It is a fact, though, that believers are almost always prevented from reaching such positions in the first place, or even entering higher education. This is very difficult to document, though it is made explicit in Party pronouncements on religion and is well known to all observers of the Soviet scene. It is mainly in the world of the arts that there are persons known to be believers active in public life, though individual instances have been reported in the scientific sphere and even the higher military command. Such political and social discrimination at a very early stage in the person's life inevitably leads to an economic discrimination as well. In effect, believers emerge as a huge group of second-class citizens throughout the Soviet Union. Such harassment and discrimination form the subject of this chapter. The cases cited are not exhaustive, but serve to give the reader some idea of what it is like to be a believer in Russia today.

The following paragraphs focus on the case of the Pentecostals, to illustrate the way discrimination is systematic. This group, alongside the Jehovah's Witnesses, Eastern Rite Catholics and some offshoots of the Orthodox Church and Old Believers, have been at various times treated as outlaws by the Soviet Government. There is no published legal basis for this, so it must be regulated by some secret decree.

Pentecostal doctrine has existed in Russia since about 1911, and grew rapidly during the immediate post-revolutionary period when they were not persecuted as a sect. By 1928 there were 200,000 Pentecostals in the USSR.[1] The name "Pentecostal" comes from the special attention they give to the day of Pentecost, when the Holy Spirit descended upon the disciples and caused them to speak with tongues. This miracle was taken as a sign that Christianity should be preached to foreign peoples. They therefore place great emphasis on proselytising, which is the primary cause of the constant persecution suffered in the USSR.

When in 1929 the Soviet Government changed its policy on religion Pentecostals were sentenced *en masse* to labour camp terms of up to ten years and in the late 1940s to terms of twenty to twenty-five years. Some were executed. Many did not return from camp. In an attempt to avoid persecution, Pentecostal communities often moved from place to place. At present there are communities from the most Western regions of the USSR including the Baltic Republics to the Far East around Vladivostok. Recently they have suffered heavily after the Government has demanded registration of all religious communities with the Council for Religious Affairs (CRA). Pentecostals were forced to register, yet the conditions of registration were often unacceptable: many of the most important areas of their religious life were banned, such as the religious education of their children, prayer groups, proselytising, philanthropic activities, and some religious ceremonies. As a result many in fact refused to register. One Pentecostal Vasily Patrushev said: "We have no choice, either we become criminals in the eyes of the Government by refusing to submit to the regulations on registration and thereby observing the teachings of Christ, or we become criminals in the eyes of God by submitting to the demands of the Government. For us, believers living according to conscience, the higher law is the law of God. We cannot become criminals before God".[2]

This incompatibility between Pentecostal religious instruction and Soviet orders also determines their lives from childhood. From the beginning of school the children must accept the enmity they encounter as members of a sect. Pentecostal children refuse to join Soviet youth organisations – the Octobrists, Pioneers, and the Komsomol. As a result their grades are lowered, they suffer public criticism at school meetings, they are beaten by other children, sometimes at the instigation of teachers. Teachers subject Pentecostal children to hostile questionings in an attempt to make them accuse their parents of forcing them to take part in religious ceremonies. If children admit to this, criminal proceedings may be started against their parents, or their children may even be taken away from them and placed in state boarding schools.

Compulsory military service is also extremely difficult for Pentecostals to accept because their doctrine forbids them to swear oaths, bear weapons, or take life. The Chronicle of Current Events in May 1977 reported that 160 Pentecostal recruits in the Rovno Region refused to serve except on construction or in medical units.[3] Higher education is rare amongst Pentecostals because of the difficult conditions they face at school. Consequently, they do not get good jobs. Many are common labourers, or work in low paid "least desirable" positions such as construction workers or watchmen. They are frequently dismissed by order of the Party leadership, and no matter how hard they work will not get promotion.

Pentecostals are also subject to considerable anti-religious propaganda which creates an atmosphere of wariness and suspicion towards them. The wife of Nikolay Goretoy, a Pentecostal bishop, relates that in the children's hospital where she worked as a cleaning woman a doctor told her: "We need someone to work in the kitchen badly, but I cannot send you there. Everyone knows you are a sect member, and people will think you are poisoning the children's food".[4] This was said to a woman who had raised fourteen children in extremely difficult circumstances! In November 1980 a young woman called Zolotova and her son were killed in Yaroslavl when their gas-stove exploded. Knowing she was a Pentecostal, the officials put out two versions of the event: that Zolotova killed herself and her son because she was a religious fanatic, or that her husband killed her and her son because he was. The night after these events, militia men broke into Zolotova's parents' home and took away the two remaining children. They were held until morning ostensibly for fear that they would be killed too.[5]

Soviet newspapers spread rumours that Pentecostals use religion to cover ulterior motives, that they are in the service of the West and are paid by the US to shelter American spies. Such stories are widely accepted, because they explain the unusual lifestyle of Pentecostals. They often live in communities, are utterly sober, and therefore appear materially better off. In films Pentecostals have been shown praying on the beach, where they go to avoid harassment from the authorities. They are depicted as waiting for an ark filled with American dollars, or to take them away to the "Promised Land". When the Pentecostal bishop Ivan Fedotov, whose activities have already been quoted in Chapter 5, received packages of clothing and gifts from fellow-believers abroad on several occasions, an article appeared in a local newspaper entitled: "Fedotov Gets Paid for Everything". It said that "the packages are nothing more than payment for slanders against his country that Fedotov has sent abroad, or an advance for which he must work up some new libel of our Soviet way of life".[6] The press also accuses sect members of shielding their children from life by forbidding them going to the cinema, dances and so forth. Young Pentecostals are committed to a life of seclusion not because of religious prohibitions, but because of the prejudices of those around them fostered by Soviet officials. When they go to social functions they are often abused and even beaten up, but in spite of this their numbers are on the increase. Their lives are seen in sharp contrast with ordinary Soviet life, with its alcoholism and spiritual emptiness. The number of Soviet Pentecostals is estimated now to be as many as one million.[7]

Perhaps as a direct result of all this discrimination and persecution the Pentecostals developed a new doctrine after the Second World War, namely the necessity of an exodus from the Soviet Union. They believe that God will lead the Jews, the Chosen People whose emigration has already begun, and the righteous, from that sinful land. A Pentecostal movement for emigration began in the spring of 1973. In 1974 contacts were made between them and the Moscow Human Rights Activists, and from 1976 information on the Pentecostals appeared regularly in the *Chronicle of Current Events*. It was published in every issue under two headings: "Persecution of Believers", and "The Right to Emigrate".

Pentecostals are still attempting to get official permission to leave the USSR. There are many examples, however, of Soviet officials harassing them in order to stop publication of their plight. Lydia Voronina, a Muscovite visiting the communities in Nakhodka and Starotitarovskaya to get a picture of the situation on behalf of the Moscow Helinski Group, spent several days in each community talking to practically every family. She attended meetings and listened to their questions. She made a strong impression on the Pentecostals, and the support of the Moscow Human Rights Activists and contacts with the free World were seen as a possible turning point in their struggle. Voronina was followed by KGB agents during her visits, and was hauled in by them to explain the purpose of her trip. When she was leaving Nakhodka a rock was thrown at her car. The window was broken but no one was hurt. On her return to Moscow her apartment was searched and all the notes taken during the trip were confiscated. After she had left Nakhodka, registered Pentecostal leaders arrived in the town and attacked those trying to emigrate or communicate with the Moscow Helinski Group. "We must seek help from God, and not from some leftist forces", they said at a meeting.[8] For a time the authorities began to lessen repression against Pentecostals in order to head off the movement towards emigration.

The temporary lifting of restrictions has not, however, stopped the general hopes for emigration. On the election of Mr Carter as President of the USA hopes for emigration increased but came to nothing. By 1980 a letter had been addressed to President Reagan asking him to appeal to Mr Brezhnev to allow Pentecostals to leave the USSR. As far as is known, Reagan did not reply. Many Pentecostals were arrested between 1979 and 1981, both for their desire to emigrate or like Ivan Fedotov for refusing to register. But in spite of all this, Pentecostals still refuse to register, and continue to pursue an independent line.

However, let one of the best known Pentecostal families speak for themselves. This is the account of Alexander and Raisa Balak (both in their early forties), their sons Igor (b. 1964), Oleg (b. 1965), and Vitali (b. 1971), and Raisa's younger unmarried sister Lyudmila Tarasenko, who lives with them. They write as follows:

We, the Balak family applied to emigrate from the USSR in January 1978 and in August of that year renounced Soviet citizenship. Since that time our family have suffered a series of serious repressions and restrictions from the atheist authorities, who have taken matters to extremes. We have three times been obliged to change our place of residence, since we found ourselves under threat of imprisonment and even in danger of our lives. Earlier we lived in Zhdanov, on the right bank, fourth Azovsky Street, house 12.

When we applied to emigrate on the grounds of religious convictions, the authorities tried to persuade us to stay by offering us a flat, money, carpets, all sorts of benefits imaginable. When the "carrot" proved unsuccessful, the stick was in turn applied with all its cruelty. Our neighbours were set against us and we were constantly shadowed. Our children were beaten in our own yard by grown-up neighbours, who also attacked us adults in groups.

The militia refused to take any steps, saying, "You are not our citizens". We were tormented by constant visits from the militia, the regional executive committee and the school administration. Everything was done to make our life unbearable. But the authorities went even further in their lawlessness and arbitrariness. When our son Oleg was thirteen, he was given a poisoned cutlet and macaroni to eat at school. For three days the boy was close to death; he had a temperature of 40°C vomited unceasingly and began to go into convulsions. Only through our prayers did God preserve his life. When I informed the headmistress of the school of the above facts and prohibited my children from eating at school, the headmistress, L. V. Chelyabina, was not in the least surprised, but asked in return: "How did he survive? Not by your prayers – he simply had a strong healthy body". Our sheepdog which had prevented the militia from making surprise raids on our home had shortly before that been poisoned in the same way. Our lives were under serious threat. The Procurator of Zhdanov, Comrade Breier, told us to get out, otherwise our house would be bulldozed.

In 1980 we had to leave Zhdanov and move into the Krasnopolye settlement, in Sumy region. We acquired a site in order to build a house. But the authorities there would not leave us in peace either. All the craftsmen in the district were warned and frightened off by the investigating authorities, and refused to build our house. The building of the house was completed with great difficulty, using what abilities we had. We put all our energy and financial means into that house but were never able to live in it. The authorities set the local community against us, saying things like, "they are criminals, going from town to town killing people". In the furniture factory where we worked deliberately intolerable conditions were created for us. The chairman of the comrades court informed us that we were being evicted as an undesirable element and we would be isolated from the community. Things became so serious and threatening that we did not wait for threats to be carried out, and were obliged to leave Sumy region. We were not able to sell our house. The general director of the wood-processing plant, comrade M. N. Grishko, told us that the Soviet authorities would decide whether or not our house would be sold, although no-one had told him anything about the sale of the house. Evidently the Soviet authorities had decided that we should get by without a roof over our heads at all. Our whole family moved to Krasnodar region.

We rented a flat, but were not left in peace here either, and new difficulties overtook us. Our son Oleg entered the professional-technical college number thirty in September 1981. After studying four and a half months, he decided to leave his studies and go to work, attending evening school to learn a trade according to his liking. But it turned out that our children do not have the right to choose a profession. They must act only according to the whims of the higher organs of power. We found work for Oleg in a jam works, signed an application for work and had him accepted, but the district executive committee would not allow Oleg to start work.

The reason given, in the words of the first secretary of the Party committee, comrade N. V. Polovnoy, was that "the college cannot release your son because it is essential that he be re-educated in the spirit of atheism, whereas at work they will be unable to give him the same attention". Every effort was made to force him to study. And when all this proved unsuccessful the college director arranged for the foreman, comrade V. M. Malakhov, to go to our home and notify us that Oleg would not be taken out of the jam works because "the works director has already changed his mind about taking him, and you must pay six to seven hundred roubles for four and a half months study at the college". The result, therefore, was the college would not release him, but was presenting a bill, Oleg was not allowed to start work, and the college director and the chairman of the district executive committee threatened us parents with legal action because our son was neither studying nor working.

We appealed to the Presidium of the USSR Supreme Soviet and the All-Union Visa and Registration Department of the Ministry of Internal Affairs requesting that the authorities give attention to the harassment and oppressive treatment that we had received simply because of our religious beliefs. There was no place for us in the town or the village, and in our hopeless situation we asked that our application for emigration be promptly considered. A month later we were told that our request had been passed to the Krasnodar region executive committee for a decision. They in turn passed us on to the Abinsk district executive committee. The deputy chairman, comrade Koreshkov, refused to allow Oleg to start work and two days later demanded payment of the fine because he was neither studying nor working. In order to avert further complaints and to get rid of us, the district executive committee sent a directive to the militia to deal with us.

At 11 pm on 16 April 1982 the divisional inspector, Lieutenant Puslavsky, called on us and demanded our passports. When we refused to hand them over, he told us to take them to the militia department and added that in a week "there should not be a trace of you here; you have a week, otherwise we will arrest you as vagrants".[9]

A further very important example of discrimination and harassment exercised against religion in ordinary life is the almost total lack of publicly available religious literature. Looking at this from the viewpoint of the West it is hard to imagine what life would be like without access to religious books. The fact is that in the USSR, apart from the *Journal of the Moscow Patriarchate*, the Baptist *Fraternal Herald*, and one or two other regular publications no religious literature may be published. There are the occasional printings of the Bible or New Testament, but the JMP has a very limited circulation and, of course, only represents the Orthodox Church. Together with this it only rarely finds its way into the hands of ordinary believers. Thus there is no means of finding out about faith except through *samizdat*.

*Samizdat* is a very simple process. The author types his work on to a typewriter (difficult to obtain but the only means at the disposal of the average Soviet citizen), makes four or five carbon copies and passes these on to other interested people. They in turn will make copies and distribute them. The more successful the work, the faster and further it will be distributed. *Samizdat* is extremely inefficient in terms of time and effort, but it is the only possible way of overcoming the government monopoly on ideas and information. It has attracted talented writers, fearless and energetic distributors, and a readership that is continually growing. Those who hunger for a truthful picture of the world and for genuine knowledge are prepared to sacrifice time and energy and even persecution for its sake. Russian *samizdat* began with poetry. By the late 1950s and early 1960s, essays, short stories and articles were circularised in *samizdat*. Some like the poet Yevtushenko were officially approved. Others like Joseph Brodsky were not. Vladimir Bukovsky says that at that time all the typewriters in Moscow were in total demand. A youth culture grew up whose password was a knowledge of poetry, Pasternak, and Mandelshtam. Former prisoners wrote of their experiences and Pasternak's *Dr Zhivago* was one of the first books to be widely distributed in *samizdat*. But a popular book written in *samizdat* was only available to the reader for a short time because of the waiting list. Often entire families would stay up all night reading or would invite friends over for a collective reading. People would sit next to each other, passing the pages along, or read the works aloud or project microfilm copies onto a wall. *Samizdat* preserved Russian literature for Russia and for the world, and also contributed to the self-knowledge of Soviet society and the formation of an historical perspective of its present and future. The exchange of ideas through *samizdat* helped both author and reader to form their ideas about possible change in Soviet society.

There was one other way of disseminating information and that was to construct an illegal printing press. There are many examples of this. One of the best known is the press set up by the True and Free Seventh Day Adventists in the mid 1970s. This underground publishing house was called True Witness, and published religious literature and works on human rights. The KGB made immediate attempts to liquidate it and started to investigate its contributors as well as trying to discover the whereabouts of the press. They persecuted many members of the sect and attempted without success to extract information from them. Just what they had to endure is clear from the report of a 19-year-old Adventist Yakov Dolgoter. He was stopped by the KGB in February 1978 and found to be carrying pamphlets published by the True Witness. He was detained for a month while investigators tried to find out where he had got them. Two KGB agents were assigned to the investigation. "They beat me by turns, first one then the other. They beat me on the head, the face, the jaw; they beat me on the neck, being careful to raise the collar of my shirt each time so that there would be no mark. They beat me under the ribs and near my kidneys, each time swearing and repeating: 'tell us where you got it and who gave it to you, or we will show you what Soviet power is'. They suspended me by the neck with a scarf and beat me under the ribs, several times they beat me unconscious and then revived me with cold water". After three days of this they threw Dolgoter into a cold room full of bedbugs, and the next morning took him to a psychiatric hospital where the doctor asked him the same questions. They then said they would declare him to be insane. They threatened him with the arrest of his father, with the electric chair, with castration, and with a long prison sentence. A month later, having found out nothing, they released him. On 20 March 1978 he reported what had happened to foreign correspondents in Moscow and was later rearrested. He was convicted for organising an underground press and given a four-year prison sentence.[10]

This illustrates the desperate lengths that people have to go in order to publish religious literature in the USSR at all; and how precious that literature becomes as it passes from hand to hand. This struggle for what we in the West take entirely for granted is eloquently summed up in a defence speech made by a 25-year-old Adventist Nina Ovcharenko on 15 October 1979: "Everyone has the right, as a complete individual endowed with all rights and liberties from birth, to his own beliefs. This right is enshrined in Article 19 of the Declaration of Human Rights and the International Pacts on Human Rights ratified by our Government in 1957 and 1963. All laws, both International and State, guarantee freedom of conscience for all. This is the most fundamental, and most important right of all; it makes every citizen a free and complete human being. The lack of freedom of conscience deprives a man of dignity and reduces him to the state of an animal, having only the right to work and rest. Truth and justice are not always on the side of the majority. I consider myself a happy person because I am a part of the struggle for truth".[11]

The KGB are continually on the lookout for illegal printing presses, and are often successful in tracking them down. They discovered the whereabouts of another one in October 1985. It was found in the home of Georgi and Mariya Rotaru, who are unregistered Baptists and live in the village of Staraya Obrezha near the town of Beltsy in Moldavia, not far from the Soviet Union's border with Romania. Six arrests were made, though it was reported that as many as ten people were involved, including several from registered churches. The raid was made while the press was actually in operation, and the authorities confiscated all the equipment including a portable printing press and five tons of paper. The press was publishing copies of the New Testament in Moldavian, and these were also taken.[12]

As for pressure, there are many different kinds that can be applied to believers. First there is what can be called general pressure. This is well illustrated in the case of Father Pavel Lysak, an Orthodox priest from the Ukraine. He had wanted to enter the priesthood from boyhood, and graduated from high school with honours but was denied the gold medal because he refused to join the Communist Youth League, the Komsomol. After school he was called up to do his military service and managed to remain faithful to his Church and at the same time do well at his military training, receiving forty-seven commendations. Afterwards he entered the Odessa Seminary and in 1970 was tonsured as a monk and consecrated a deacon. He was accepted for the Moscow Theological Academy and settled in the Trinity St Sergius Monastery at Zagorsk. His piety soon drew people to him, and inevitably it was not long before the KGB took an interest in him as well. In 1975 Father Pavel was expelled from St Sergius monastery, and deprived of the right to live anywhere in the Moscow region. He was ordered to leave within seventy-two hours. From then on his life became one of wandering, persecution, slander and humiliation, all of which, according to the people who knew him, he bore with considerable courage and patience.

Friends came to Father Pavel's aid and he got a residence permit for the town of Kimry in the Kalinin region. Yet as his popularity grew here the KGB unleashed a vicious tide of slanderous rumours about him. They put it out that he was a black-marketeer, a homosexual, a perverter of minors and so forth. But the faithful simply ignored them, and all the local KGB had to show at the end of seven years of effort was a dossier of alleged complaints about the "anti-Soviet leanings" of Father Pavel, and hints that "he is popular among the Jews". The KGB had to resort to the depositions of a number of active atheists to the effect that Father Pavel was a "religious fanatic" who was influencing young people in favour of religion.

In 1983 a young and energetic KGB officer called

A. Makarov was placed in charge of investigating Father Pavel. Under his direction "young hooligans" staged a number of attacks on the flat in which he stayed when travelling up to Moscow to see friends. During Lent 1984 Makarov's men managed to trick their way into the flat claiming that there was someone in urgent need of a priest. Once inside Makarov drew a gun and threatened everyone while rooms were ransacked in a fruitless search for incriminating evidence. When nothing was found Makarov forced Father Pavel to sign an undertaking that he would leave Moscow immediately. During the next months Father Pavel's Moscow friends were questioned by the KGB, who tried by threats and bribery to secure evidence against him. No one, however, yielded to this "general pressure". In order to bring charges against a monk in accordance with Soviet law Makarov needed two signed undertakings by Father Pavel that he would leave Moscow, and he only had one.

On 3 August 1984 Makarov learned that Father Pavel was in Moscow again, and the next day together with his "operational group" he once more managed to trick his way into the flat where Father Pavel was staying. This time a woman "operative", poorly dressed and swathed in a headscarf tearfully pleaded to be let into the flat to see the Father. As soon as the door was opened Makarov and his men burst in and turned it upside down in their search for evidence. Their haul consisted of several Bibles, two prayer-books and one Soviet-produced record of Easter hymns. Makarov forced a woman neighbour to accompany him back to headquarters where he subjected her to many hours of questioning and threats until she was intimidated into writing and signing a statement dictated to her by him. All her subsequent efforts to withdraw this statement, as one which was untrue and obtained under duress, were turned down by the various official bodies she approached. At the trial, to which she was summoned as a witness for the prosecution, she was reviled by the judge who refused to allow her to retract her statement. Despite her protests it was retained as a part of the evidence against Father Pavel.

Another document fabricated by Makarov purported to come from one Sergei Medvedev and stated that he had "regularly delivered food" to Father Pavel at the named address; the aim being to try and prove that Father Pavel was living permanently in Moscow. It emerged that the real Sergei Medvedev had been in prison for theft since January 1984! Incredible as it may seem, even to those accustomed to the peculiar twists of "socialist legality", this patently unacceptable document was also one of the bases for the charges against Father Pavel. The investigation was every bit as questionable as Makarov's evidence, but as Father Pavel's friends pointed out the outcome of the trial had already decided by the KGB in advance. On 4 December 1984 Father Pavel was sentenced to ten months' deprivation of freedom for "violating internal passport regulations".[13]

There is a good deal of evidence of general pressure such as I have described, but another point is that harassment continues even after a prisoner is released. One of the major difficulties is getting work. Dr Viktor Brailovsky, for example, recently returned from a five year term in exile, and is experiencing new problems in Moscow. Brailovsky, who was sentenced in 1980 for editing a Jewish *samizdat* journal, was allowed to register at his old address after completing his exile on 15 March 1984. However, he is now being pressured by the police to find work. Brailovsky is doing everything he can to find a job but as yet has not succeeded. He apparently applied for a job as a lift attendant, but when his potential employers learnt that he had a "criminal record" they found a pretext for refusing him. Dr Brailovsky is a cyberneticist,[14] cannot find work in this field, and when he tries for unskilled work he is told he is over-qualified. He and his wife are taking the police pressure and threats very seriously as they know that with a conviction behind him he is particularly vulnerable.[15] If he does not find work soon he could well be arrested for "parasitism".

There are, however, *specific* ways in which believers are harassed and discriminated against. The first of these is the continual barrage of atheistic propaganda. Believers can be slandered in the press and on the radio without any right of reply. There are numerous instances of this; here is one example, quoted from the *Evangelical Times*:

> "The anti-religious campaign being waged by the government-controlled Soviet media is turning even more vicious towards unofficial Baptist Churches", claims Brother Andrew. "Baptists are being falsely accused in print of murder, sadism and fanaticism, as part of a plan to discredit this group of Christians. One publication *Trud* (Labour), purports to describe how a member of an unregistered Baptist congregation had murdered his wife after 45 years of marriage. Other articles have depicted young Baptists as sadists and fanatics. The tactic is not new, and its emergence is hardly a surprise.[16]

The Soviet Government's concern that atheistic propaganda retains the upper hand in the battle for young minds is seen in the first major press article on religion to be published in *Pravda* since Mr Gorbachev came to power. This was written on 13 September 1985 by Dr R. Platonov, Director of the Party's History Institute in the Republic of Byelorussia. He is concerned that the Russian Orthodox Church will be celebrating its 1,000th anniversary of Christianity in Russia in 1988. The scope of the planned festivities has not yet been announced, but the authorities are plainly worried about the possible effect on the morale of atheists. Dr Platonov calls for an urgent reappraisal of current methods of atheistic propaganda. These, he suggests, are now proving inadequate to deal with the evolving intellectual and spiritual demands of the Soviet people. Dr Platonov somewhat defensively quotes the proportion of practising believers in towns as a mere 8–10%, (Keston College points out that many atheists admit 20%), whereas the proportion for rural areas is somewhat higher, although he gives no figures. He nevertheless insists that atheist propaganda must be forcefully directed to counter religious activity, and to galvanise the passively atheistic sector of the population.

Dr Platonov warns of threats from militant clerical circles and from the West which, he claims, is already exploiting the Orthodox Millenium to stir up political unrest. However, he also states that serious thought must be given to the more sophisticated intellectual believer whose presence has become disturbingly evident in Soviet society in recent years. Religious intellectualism is dangerous because it purports to reconcile science and social ideology with religious faith. It bears the marks of realism and patriotism, whereas in fact, Dr Platonov declares, it is nothing but a destructive sham. Nevertheless, Dr Platonov is concerned that atheist propaganda should respond more effectively to questions put by the religiously inclined, and present Marxism–Leninism as a credible substitute for religious faith, which he regards as primitive superstition. Atheist propaganda should be directed particularly at the young, to discourage receptivity to any religious influences from the home. He adds that atheist agitators must be rigorously selected and trained. They must also have comprehensive knowledge of the social environment in which they operate, understand it, and expect to live and work in it.[17] We in the West may wonder to what degree the celebrations of the Millenium will be allowed to go ahead, and what kind of message about the true state of the Russian Orthodox Church they will ultimately carry to the rest of the world.

It is amusing to see that in recent months there has been concern expressed in the Soviet media about the use of religious and similar "archaic" terminology in everyday Russian language, both spoken and printed. A typical example of this is reflected in the Soviet journalists' professional publication *Zhurnalist*, No 6, 1985. "I did not have to look for examples", writes the author B. Stepanov, "It is enough to cast a casual glance at any periodical publication, to see numerous unnecessary usage of archaic terminology, biblical symbolism, and pious sayings and figures of speech". All too often, laments Stepanov: "the utterings of Kolkhoz Chairmen and similar heroes of 'paper and journal articles are a mixture of terminology of the technical epoch with mentions of God, religious oaths, references to fate and providence. Without a trace of irony they speak about the mysteries of the human psyche, premonitions, prophetic dreams, they discuss auspicious colours of the Year of the Horse or the Monkey and casually greet women working in the fields with the words 'May God speed you, girls' "![18] There have been campaigns in the past to "purge" the language of all religious connotations, but they have usually been short-lived and unsuccessful. The rebuke cited by Lenin: "you are atheists on the surface, while God remains in your hearts", is certainly true for the population at large, if not for the propagandists of atheism.

Closely related to atheist propaganda is the importance given to the teaching of atheism in Soviet schools. The number of believers teaching in schools is very small indeed, and they will have no chance of promotion. Children of believers will also experience problems at school. They will have to attend compulsory classes on atheism, while the teaching of religion is banned. The timetable is thus slanted towards atheism, and the Soviet Government's concern to promote atheist education can be seen from a letter written by a believing schoolgirl to *The Chronicle of the Lithuanian Catholic Church*:

> When I was in the 4th grade, from the beginning of the school year my homeroom teacher insisted that I join the Pioneers. All 4th grade pupils had to be Pioneers. But I never joined. My homeroom teacher said that if I did not join this year, I certainly must next. He threatened me with lower grades and other unpleasantness if I did not. Truly, that is how it was. Some teachers consistently gave me lower grades. My homeroom teacher frequently saw me going to church in the evenings. Once he asked me where I went every evening. I answered that

I attend church. After that he used every opportunity to stress, "Once and for all, stop this going to church"! Questionnaires were distributed in class with questions such as: "Do you attend church? Where did human beings come from: from a monkey or from God? Who forces you to attend church? Do you celebrate religious holidays? Does the church harm or help?"

I answered, "I attend church. God created human beings. I attend church of my own will. We celebrate religious holidays. The church does only good".

Once my homeroom teacher called me in and said: "I know that you attend church. Well, then, attend! But when the commission arrives and asks you whether you attend, whether you believe, then say that you do not attend and do not believe". At home my parents advised me never to renounce or foreswear God. In class we were frequently required to write atheistic themes. In this way my homeroom teacher persecuted me for my beliefs until the end of the school year.[19]

The aims of Soviet atheist education are made clear in an article in the Soviet weekly magazine *Nauka i religiya* (Science and Religion) in which the author, L. Fyodorova, discusses the process of atheist education in the schools of the town of Pechory, near Pskov. The writer appears to be a local party worker or an employee of the Department of Education. She writes: "Anyone who comes to this district cannot fail to notice the abundance of 'cult' buildings and the many functioning religious establishments; for example, there are the monastery, 14 Russian Orthodox Churches, a Lutheran Church, and two prayer houses for the Evangelical Baptists. There are parents who try to involve their children in religion and for this reason atheist educational work in schools carries special significance".[20]

In the field of education, regular meetings, seminars and conferences are held for teachers of all descriptions whose task it is to introduce atheist ideas irrespective of the subject being taught. Some teachers are involved in atheist work as an extra-curricular activity and will have completed a correspondence course specifically on the subject of atheism.

Teachers must explain during lessons for the younger children the harmful effects of religious superstitions, as well as the unsoundness and absurdity of religion. For older children, the history, biology and geography lessons are vehicles for stronger atheist work where materials and teaching aids are used.

A great deal of atheist work is done outside the classroom in the schools' atheist clubs. The most active and able of the senior children are selected to give talks to the younger classes. Scientific experiments are used to disprove religious miracles. Meetings are frequently held to discuss the latest books propagating the atheist message. Teachers are asked to pay special attention to the children of religious parents. Quite often these parents do not allow their children to become young Octobrists or Pioneers, or members of the Komsomol, the Young Communist League, in their teens.

The influence of the home is still the most important reason why belief remains strong in the Soviet Union. The authorities are plainly worried by this fact. Newspaper articles show how anti-religious writers try hard to exploit family disagreements over religion. One such example tells how a N. Mikhailova and the chairman for the local council for atheist education visited a middle-aged couple who live in Maisiagala near Vilnius. Their story illustrates the problems of school children brought up in the homes of believers. According to them the couple's elder daughter ruined her school career when she allowed her mother to persuade her to join a church choir. Until then the daughter had been getting on well at school and was respected by her fellow pupils. Soon afterwards, they say, she lost interest in her studies, leaving school and home.[21]

On the other hand, teachers in Bukhara think that the real solution lies in starting atheist education from the moment a child enters school. They complain that in its present form atheist education is not making a deep impact. For example, they report that one pupil of the fifth class in the school No 6 does not believe in God when he is at school, but does when he goes home according to the results of a questionnaire![22] It is, therefore, impossible to give any really clear idea of the effect of atheist education in schools, but the Government certainly have all the advantages on their side.

So far we have been showing how the authorities discriminate against believers by putting a one-sided view of religion without the right of reply. But believers are also physically and mentally harassed in other ways. One of the most alarming is to be subjected to a house search. It is bad enough in this country to return home to find a burglar has ransacked your house, but in the Soviet Union this is used as a deliberate technique to harass believers. There are innumerable examples of it, all of which follow a similar pattern. This example concerns Father Gleb Yakunin already mentioned in chapter 3, and is part of his report to the *Christian Committee for the Defence of Believers' Rights in the USSR*.

On 28 September 1979 a search lasting for 12 hours was carried out at my flat by the KGB operatives, Major Yakovlev, Kireyev and Finogenov, in connection with case No 12 of the Leningrad directorate of the KGB (the case of the *samizdat* journal *Community*, which is being conducted by the investigator for Cases of Special Importance, Major Lepetunov, in which the accused is Vladimir Poresh, a member of the young peoples' Christian Seminar founded by A. Ogorodnikov).

In connection with the events of the search I consider it necessary to declare the following:
1. Among the things confiscated during the search was the archive of the "Christian Committee", as well as materials connected with its continuing work. The real aim of the search was to strike a blow against the work of the CCDBR, to hinder its activities, and possibly in preparation for further repressive measures.
2. CCDBR has repeatedly called the World's attention to the frequent incidents of the confiscation of purely religious literature during such searches. Nor would this incident have been

complete without the confiscation of such material. In particular, among the books taken were the following editions of the Brussels-based Catholic publishing house "Life with God": E. Svetlov, *The Heralds of the Kingdom of God* 1978. S. Bolshakov *On the Heights of the Spirit* 1971. The *Akathists* (an Orthodox prayer book) 1978. (This is our "freedom" to conduct the religious cult!).

3. During the search 4 account deposit books were confiscated, representing a total sum of 1,589 roubles, belonging to an Orthodox Christian and resident of the City of Krasnoyarsk, Grigori Vladimirovich Mitasov, who had deposited these savings in my name for promotion of the Christian religious renaissance.

After the search the investigator, Major Yakovlev, refused to allow us to add a written protest to the protocol on the pretext that this would "spoil the protocol". My wife and I refused to sign the protocol of the search. Signed G. Yakunin, Priest. 10 October 1979.[23]

There is also considerable harassment of Baptists who contravene the laws on Religious Associations. Baptist weddings are traditionally large because of the custom of inviting the entire religious community, and often neighbouring communities as well, and are liable to spill out into the garden or yard. In the larger communities the guests run into hundreds and a private home cannot contain them. Yet, according to the instructions of the Government's Council for Religious Affairs, "ritual assemblies" may not be held in the open air. And so it is not a rare occurrence for Baptist weddings to be dispersed.

On 15 May 1977 at the home of dissenting Baptist M. A. Boyev a daughter's wedding was being celebrated. On the day of the wedding the local authorities hung a sign by the approach to the house: "Quarantine. Passage Prohibited for Pedestrians and Vehicles". Then the electricity supply to the house was cut off, and as a result the orchestra was unable to play. Near the house officials of the KGB, the district Soviet executive committee, and the police assembled, altogether several dozen people. When the ritual singing began and the bride and groom came out into the garden, the chairman of the village Soviet began to make out an order about the violation of public order, and went about taking the names of all those present. The believers and the Boyevs' neighbours tried to explain to him that he had no reason to do this. Police officials asked the people who had gathered in the garden and at the fence around the house to disperse, and began to talk and laugh loudly. Then a bulldozer drove up to the house and stopped with its engine still going, drowning the sermon. The KGB men began to photograph believers. The latter in turn began to photograph the bulldozer. It was removed, the officials themselves then tried to avoid being photographed.[24]

It is also common for Baptists to organise youth outings in the countryside, and harvest festivals are often celebrated by several communities together. These are, however, prohibited. Here is a description of one such youth outing:

Young Baptists in the Omsk, Kokchetav and Tselinograd regions decided to hold a united open air service on Sunday 4 June 1977 in a forest in Isil'kul district. The day before the traffic police had already blocked all approaches to the place where the service was to be held and were turning cars away, checking the documents of drivers, and taking their numbers and fining them. Those who managed to reach the place held a service for about two hours in relative peace, but then the clearing in the forest was surrounded and tractors brought up. These began to tear up the ground, trying to run people over and drowning the prayers with the noise of their powerful engines. In the end police and vigilantes began to provoke a fight. Despite the fact that the believers did not physically resist, the police filled the Black Marias with those arrested and drove them to the police station, where they were detained until the evening. The rest were dispersed with insults and violence: rough wrestling methods were used – they were dragged along by the hair, beaten with sticks, and threatened with firearms. The food, dishes and other things which had been prepared for the supper were confiscated and taken away. The tractors broke down the shrubs and saplings while chasing through the wood after the Baptists. Many of the vigilantes were drunk.[25]

In the last chapter we mentioned conscription for all men over eighteen and saw that many Baptists were prepared to give up the time but were not willing to undergo military training or take the oath. Instead they wanted to offer themselves for work in hospitals and other duties which would not involve fighting. This, however, is not allowed and so many young Christians find themselves subjected to harassment in the form of mental and physical torture carried out by the authorities and other soldiers. One such case is Misha Naiden who was due to take the military oath on 20 December 1983. He refused and was then ordered by his commanding officer to explain himself to all those present for the ceremony. This included parents, older soldiers and other important people. The hope was that Naiden might be shamed into compliance. Instead he took the opportunity to explain the reasons for his refusal and to witness to Christ. As a result he was put in prison for a fortnight, where he was taunted by the guards. Later, on a number of occasions, his fellow soldiers tried to kill him. Finally, he was called into a room by a number of officers, who said that they did not believe he was a real Christian and were going to carry out an experiment to test him. They said they would stick nails in his back and that if he endured the trial peacefully they would accept that his faith was real. Naiden prayed for strength and was able to withstand the nails, remaining peaceful despite terrible pain. The officers were amazed and said that they now believed him to be a real Christian. One added: "I had never thought you would be ready to die for your faith in God".[26]

Housing can also be manipulated to victimise believers. Getting a decent flat especially in the larger cities in the USSR is very difficult. Most people live in very small flats and will often have a grandmother or one of their married children living with them. Conditions are therefore very cramped with little privacy, which is thought to be one of the reasons for the high divorce rate in the Soviet Union. Most flats are owned by the local authority, who have the power to refuse registration in their area and in so doing deny accommodation. Thus the provision of housing gives the authorities many opportunities to discriminate against believers, who are not in control of their own lives and can be refused adequate housing.

Special problems can face believers who have been released from imprisonment. One such case is Jonas Sadunas, brother of Nijole Sadunaite, who is being threatened by the Soviet authorities in Vilnius, Lithuania, with eviction from the Sadunas family home. The apartment shared for the last fifteen years by Nijole, Jonas and his wife and small daughter, is registered in Nijole's name. After serving a six-year term of imprisonment in 1974–1980 for typing the *Chronicle of the Lithuanian Catholic Church*, Nijole Sadunaite was again threatened with arrest in 1982 for writing a book about her experiences in Soviet labour camps. To avoid arrest she was forced to go into hiding. Meanwhile Jonas Sadunas' family continued to live in his sister's apartment, although Jonas himself was first interned in a psychiatric hospital in 1982 and then sentenced to one and a half years' forced labour camp in 1983 for alleged slander. Since his release, Sadunas has been unable to find work.

In June 1985 the cooperative board in charge of the apartment began to take steps to evict Nijole Sadunaite from the cooperative and thus revoke her ownership, as she had "assumed permanent residence elsewhere". Jonas Sadunas then applied for membership of the cooperative and continued to live in the apartment. Legally the board should not be able to quarrel with this as no complaints had been made by the neighbours, but it seems probable that they will be forced to leave the apartment and would then be unlikely to be granted a further residence permit in

Vilnius. This would also expose Nijole herself to a charge of "parasitism" for having "no legal residence". The police have already told Jonas that she will be given a long sentence when they find her.[27]

A further effective method of harassment is for the authorities to administer a fine. This can be done for breaking the laws on Religious Associations. According to the 1966 decree on the application of the legislation on Religious Cults there are three grounds upon which someone may be fined up to fifty roubles, which are the equivalent of about a week's wages. These are failure to register a Religious Association; a violation of laws on the conduct of meetings, which could be the Baptist practice of holding services outside an authorised building; or holding a religious meeting for children.

The fifty rouble fine may not seem very much but it is for some households when repeated several times. For people who have been released from camp and are unable to get work because of their beliefs, it can be crippling. The following entry in the CPR Bulletin shows how frequently this happens. I have extracted only the actual instances of fining here, omitting the arrests, searches, trials, and other more serious items:

> Ryazan youth fined total of 170 roubles after going to meet ex-prisoner A. Kalyashin; Bryansk believers fined for presence of children at their services; dispersal of service at Bryansk-Bezhitsa with fine; A. M. Vlasenko fined 50 roubles in January 1981 and home searched in May 1981; fines of Melitopol believers; dispersal of Cheretsky meeting in April 1981 and May 1981 with fines; V. Orlov taken to militia station following dispersal of Khartsyzsk meeting in November 1981, beaten up; fines and short sentences of Khartsyzsk believers, threats against their minister V. I. Yudintsev.[28]

The final and most important form of discrimination and harassment is the lack of churches in many areas of the USSR, especially outside the major towns. It is easy for the visitor to Moscow or Leningrad to get the impression that there are plenty of open churches, and certainly when you go to them they are full. This may be so along the tourist routes, but it is not the case in the countryside. Here a believer will often have to travel very long distances to find an open church, even if he is allowed to get there. We lack precise data on the number of churches open in these areas, but we know that about two-thirds of the 20,000 or so working Orthodox churches were closed down in the Khrushchev anti-religious campaign, and that few of these have ever reopened. This shortage affects the Orthodox more than the Baptists who are often happy to take services without a church building, and who have a less formal method of worship. More details of the situation have been given in two short *samizdat* documents sent to the West recently. The first tells of a seventeenth-century Orthodox church which is to be demolished in the ancient Russian city of Borovsk in the Kaluga region. "Only three of the 39 churches which existed in the Borovsk municipality at the time of the Revolution now remain. Before the Revolution about 90% of the population consisted of Old Believers[29] who had built a large number of churches. Today the closest place for them to worship is a three-hour bus journey away. The only restoration work being carried out in the area is at the ancient monastery in Borovsk, where work began twenty years ago".[30] The second document also reports that Rovenki (Belgorod region) has only one of its pre-war Orthodox churches open and functioning, and this is virtually falling apart. An architecturally interesting church in the village of Podmoklovo is also in a similar state of neglect.[31]

The continual threat of harassment, victimisation and discrimination hanging over all believers who want to do more than simply attend a registered church, places enormous strains on the practice of religion in the Soviet Union. It is a tribute to the dedication and deep faith of Christians of all shades in the USSR that the influence of the Church is growing in spite of such difficulties.

# 7

# Punishment

Today, unlike the Stalin period when there were wholesale arrests without trial, virtually all political prisoners in the USSR are arrested, tried, sentenced under criminal law, and released at the end of their sentence. They may, however, then be re-arrested. The only exceptions to this are people confined to psychiatric hospital. Yet it is an extremely rare occurrence for a Soviet court to acquit a defendant brought to trial for his political or religious activity. In Western terms, then, these trials are "show trials".

Let us look at the stages leading up to sentencing. By the time a believer is arrested he will already have been subject to police surveillance, house searches, questionings, confiscation of literature and typewriters, and possible dismissal from his job as described in Chapter 6. He may also have been warned that if he persists in such activities he will be arrested. Under an unpublished decree made by the Presidium of the USSR Supreme Soviet on 25 December 1972, the KGB can without recourse to the courts warn a person that their behaviour is "anti-social" and harmful to state security, and can include this warning in any future criminal case against that person. They can also notify a person's place of work and get his superiors to try to "re-educate" him.[1] Yet it is also common for a dissenter to be arrested and sentenced for up to fifteen days in jail under "administrative" procedures. This can be done by a local judge for petty offences such as "wilfully disobeying a police officer", or "petty hooliganism". Others may be arrested for one or two days "on suspicion" under a provision which allows suspects to be detained for up to three days without a charge being brought.

Perhaps worse than this, however, is the power under Article 89 of the RSFSR Criminal Procedural Code to take people into custody for a period of pre-trial investigation. Officially this can only be done if a dissenter is likely to run away, but according to Article 97 of the RSFSR Criminal Procedural Code an accused person may be held for up to nine months in custody for investigation before trial. This period can be extended by special order and often is in the case of prisoners of conscience. In major cities such people are often held in Investigative Prisons of the KGB, who have special responsibility for dissenters of every sort. These prisons are overcrowded. According to Amnesty International's account of the MVD Central Investigative Prison in Riga, Latvia, in the mid-1970s it held about 5,000 inmates at a time. As there were not enough sleeping places for them all, many had to sleep on the floor.[2] Political dissidents are usually held in a cell with one or two others. Frequently one of the others will be an *agent provocateur* or informer.

Every prisoner under investigation must observe prison discipline, get up at reveille and have one hour's exercise a day. There is a peep-hole in the door of each cell, and guards peer through at frequent intervals. A light is on twenty-four hours a day and cell windows are painted over to prevent prisoners from seeing out and daylight from coming in. They are not allowed to talk to other prisoners in the corridors. Any prisoner who violates camp discipline in pre-trial custody may be put in a punishment cell for up to ten days with reduced rations. There are usually no visits allowed for dissenters under pre-trial investigation, even if that lasts for nine months.

In practice people charged under the political articles of criminal law, for example, with teaching religion to children or distributing *samizdat*, do not often deny the charges. They argue that these are not criminal acts under the USSR Constitution. In these circumstances questionings will focus on trying to persuade them to recant or confess that their actions are criminal and also on getting information about other dissenters.

The accused may see a lawyer once the preliminary investigation is completed and then has the right to examine the documents of his case with the help of the lawyer.[3] In practice prisoners of conscience often only have access to a lawyer a few days before the trial. The investigator will then draw up the case which is called the "Bill of Indictment". This consists of the substance of the case and a formal accusation which is handed over to the procurator. It is his task to decide whether or not the case should come to court. Evidence shows that dissenters are helped most at this pre-trial stage by efforts from abroad. These can sometimes prevent the case from being brought to court.

It is also known that defence lawyers who have made energetic efforts to defend a political case have had their names struck off the list. This happened to Dina Kaminskaya who was to have defended Anatoli Shcharansky in June 1978. Mrs Kaminskaya had already defended a number of prisoners of conscience including Vladimir Bukovsky in 1967. When asked by Shcharansky's mother, Mrs Kaminskaya agreed to take the case and her name was submitted to the College of Advocates. Eleven days later the Presidium of the Moscow College of Advocates expelled her from the College. Mrs Kaminskaya had been a practising lawyer for seventeen years and was now barred from further practice. From then on she was hounded by the law herself. Her husband was summoned for questioning and then dismissed from his job, their flat was searched by police, and finally she was forced to leave the USSR.[4] Similar reprisals were taken against B. A. Zolotukin, a leading Moscow lawyer who defended Alexander Ginzburg in Moscow in 1968. He made an excellent defence of Ginzburg, but was expelled from the Party, from the

Presidium of the College of Advocates, from his post as head of a legal consultative office, and finally from the College of Advocates itself. The reason given was that he adopted a non-party and non-Soviet line in his defence of Ginzburg. So he is no longer able to work as a lawyer. Most defence lawyers have negligible effect on the outcome of the trial anyway.

The actual trial will therefore be a foregone conclusion. Trials are played down. They will not be reported in the Soviet press. The public and even families of the accused are discouraged from attending. One way of doing this is to call them as witnesses late in the trial, and as no witness can be in the courtroom until called they are effectively removed from the proceedings. Trials of religious dissidents usually last for less than a week, and are sometimes as short as just one day. This is pitiful when one considers the severity of the sentences. Much of this time will be spent reading the charges, summing up by the prosecution and defence, and only a limited time on examination of evidence.

However, accounts of some trials have found their way into *samizdat*. The period immediately after arrest and before sentence remains for many prisoners the psychologically most difficult time of their imprisonment. Isolation from family and friends, overcrowding in the cells, attacks and robberies by criminal prisoners, and tiring interrogations lead to a loss of ability to think rationally, confusion and even despair. The KGB may well cash in on this and offer a dissenter a minimal sentence or even freedom in exchange for collaboration, while the interrogator attempts of course to exploit the prisoner's unease to extract a confession.

Sentencing will involve either fining or depriving an individual of his liberty. The latter may be for a maximum of fifteen years. The court will stipulate which of five forms it will take.

The most severe is prison itself. It is rare for believers to be sent to prison for the first offence, but they may be

committed for the first part of their term while the rest will
be served in a labour camp. The second most severe institution is a Corrective Labour Colony with Special Regime.
People who are regarded by the State as especially dangerous are sent there, and this will include believers who have
offended against Article 70 of the RSFSR Criminal Code
"anti-Soviet agitation and propaganda". The third form is
an Ordinary Regime Colony. This is reserved for first
offenders, and is less severe. Fourthly there is exile to a
specified locality within the USSR, for which the maximum
sentence is five years. Exile can be imposed as a basic
punishment in addition to a sentence in prison. Lastly there
is banishment, but in practice this does not affect believers.

It is possible to appeal against a sentence, but it is fair to
say very few appeals end in altering the verdict of the court.
And in practice most prisoners end up serving the full term
of their sentence.

What are the aims of Corrective Labour Legislation? The
principles are laid down in a law approved in July 1969 by
the USSR Supreme Soviet called Fundamentals of Corrective Labour Legislation of the USSR and the Union Republics. This law replaced the anarchy which prevailed in the
Corrective Labour System under Stalin, and framed sentences into a respectable looking legal code. The two main
aims were to be the negative one of inflicting suffering, and
the positive one of reformation. The negative side of the
sentence meant the person should be "deprived of liberty",
and at the same time kept in a permanent state of hunger.
Article 56 of the RSFSR Corrective Labour Code legalises
the providing of prisoners with only that amount of food
that is biologically necessary. It is supported by Article 20
which states that those who do not fulfil their work norms
will receive the minimum necessary food. The reformative
side comprises "correction and re-education". In this regard Article 20 states: "Punishment is not only chastise-
ment for crime but also has as a goal the correction and
re-education of convicted persons in the spirit of an honest

attitude of work, exact compliance with the laws, respect for the rules of Socialist public life".

Thus according to the law "political education" must be conducted with every prisoner. Once a week he will have to attend classes. These may last up to two hours, during which current affairs, political news, and officially approved topics will be expounded. By all accounts these classes are presented badly and are resented by political prisoners, many of whom are highly educated. Eduard Kuznetsov wrote the following while serving a fifteen-year sentence in a special regime camp: "received my third reprimand for not attending political study classes. At the last class I went to Lieutenant Bezzubov gave us the priceless information that 'in China the Zionists and the Red Guards are on the rampage. But the Chinese people are not stupid, they'll show them'! The academic level of these lectures is truly breathtaking".[5] However, if prisoners followed Kuznetsov's example none of them would get an early release.

Camp administrators do not often try to re-educate religious prisoners. Yet they have a bad time in other ways. Their Bible is confiscated and they are forbidden to have any religious literature with them. And if they rebel against the camp discipline they are subject to vicious punishment.

We should now look at what happens to a prisoner once sentenced to a Corrective Labour Institution. Transportation to and from prisons and camps and into exile is thought to be one of the worst aspects of imprisonment. Broken limbs as well as heart attacks have been suffered during journeys in uncomfortable, overcrowded and poorly ventilated prison vans called black ravens (*voronki*). Prisoners sit on a bench running round three sides of the passenger compartment, and in addition the *voronok* has two tiny booths in which "especially dangerous" prisoners are placed. The vehicle is built to hold eleven passengers at the most, but often will carry twice that number. The *voronok* has metal fittings and so journeys over rough ground in country areas will inevitably result in injury.

If a prisoner has to travel a long distance to camp he will go by train in special railway cars added to the normal rail traffic, known as "Stolypin Wagons".[6] From the outside they look just like an ordinary railway carriage, but the inside has been converted into a prison cell. A Stolypin wagon has ten compartments which are designed to hold about fifty people, but in practice many more will be forced in. The toilet is at the end of the corridor and the guards will take the prisoners there one by one twice a day. Should anyone need to go more often he has to ask special permission. Thus prisoners are totally at the mercy of the guards. They also suffer from a lack of water and proper feeding arrangements for a long journey, which is particularly difficult in the summer months when the wagons get over-heated. Trains will move slowly from station to station with frequent stops. Then the wagons are put into sidings and all the windows have to be kept shut.

Sometimes prisoners will be put into transit prisons between stages of a very long journey. Georgi Davidov, a Leningrad geological engineer sentenced in 1973 to seven years' imprisonment, tells us that he was kept in a death cell in a prison in Kirov whilst in transit from his Perm camp to Vladimir in 1974. According to Davidov another prisoner was awaiting execution in a nearby cell. Every day many prisoners are routed through Moscow, a central point in the Soviet rail system, for destinations in other parts of the country. The routing usually happens at night. The inmates are taken from their temporary prisons to trains and the basements of such Moscow train stations as "Kazan", "Severnyi" (North), and "Leningrad" are used as prisons for those awaiting transport to another penal facility. The average Muscovite is unaware of the existence of these prisons.

Janis Rozkalns, a Baptist from Latvia sentenced to five years' Strict Regime Camp and three years' exile in 1983, wrote to his wife about the journey from Riga to the political camp No. 37 in the Perm region of the Urals:

> In January 1984 we began our journey to the political prisoners' camp. After lengthy travel in a caged railway wagon, we arrived at Pskov prison and were placed in cells, with barred windows and no glass. The filth was indescribable. An open lavatory bucket stood in the midst of the cell. The walls and ceiling constantly dripped water and draughts reached every corner. When we awoke during the night, covered in insect bites, our boots were floating around us. Leeches, bedbugs and earwigs were everywhere. Despite the severe frost outside, we had not so much as one blanket for covering. I asked the guard for help, pointing out that I had had tuberculosis, a fact noted in my documents. His reply was that he could do nothing. The days went by, and illnesses occurred. After 1½ weeks we were moved to another cell. There was a constant stream of hot water along the floor, and the cell was full of steam. Ten days later we spent 48 hours in transit: constant draughts, with hunks of bread and cold water as our only sustenance. The next prison in which we made a stop brought a surprise – I was forced into a shower-room with a number of mentally ill detainees. After this I was held for two weeks in an unheated isolation cell. This was followed by four days of transportation in a prisoners' railway wagon: bare floors, biting cold draughts.
>
> Upon arrival in prison in Perm, I was placed in a basement cell. My health had begun to deteriorate noticeably by this time, and I asked for medical aid. Three days later, and only after one of my fellow-prisoners threatened to go on a protest hunger-strike, did a nurse appear and hand me several tablets through a grille of the cell door. By this time I was running a high temperature and sweating profusely, but was not permitted to change my clothes. The nurse stated that the issue of blankets was limited to one, and that the prison administration refused to allow my transfer to the infirmary. It took me days finally to gain permission to be X-rayed. The diagnosis: severe pneumonia. Despite this, I was not given any warm clothing or injections for two weeks. Moreover, every day saw a rather strange inspection: several prison officers with guard-dogs would enter the cell. We would be hustled out into the

corridor, and told to kneel with our faces to the wall. In the meantime, the guards went around the cell, banging on the walls and bunks with large wooden mallets.

On 6 March 1984 I arrived at camp No 37. But even here I was unable to receive dietary food or medical treatment of any kind for a week.

All that I went through leads me to the conclusion that the trial, the transportation and the conditions in the camps are a carefully devised scheme with one aim – to break the prisoner, if not mentally, then at least physically.[7]

In his prison diaries, Kuznetsov remarks bitterly: "On the dawn of the Revolution they were going to destroy all churches and prisons. As far as the churches are concerned they seem to have done the job fairly thoroughly, but something must have gone terribly wrong when they started demolishing the prisons".[8]

On Moscow's Dzerzhinsky Square directly across from the Dzerzhinskaya Metro Station stand two semi-detached buildings joined together to form a whole. They are the Headquarters of the KGB of the USSR and the cells of its special prison the Lubyanka. The older building on the left consists of four floors. The rooms on the top floor of the new building on the right are blocked off from the outside world. Prison cells are located directly under Dzerzhinsky Square where Muscovites walk every day. A prison court-yard, enclosed by a high balustrade, is maintained on the roof. Architectural adornments on the corners of the building complex conceal watchtowers manned by soldiers with machine guns. The exact capacity of the prison is unknown, but it is estimated that half of the 200 cells were built to accommodate four inmates each. The other half are solitary confinement cells. Now only prisoners of special interest to the KGB are brought to the Lubyanka. Two especially well-known prisoners here were Solzhenitsyn and Stalin's Head of the KGB Lavrenti Beria. One of the strictest prisons in the USSR is Lefortovo, which is located in Moscow's Baumansky City district on Aerodinamicheskaya Street next to the Central Aerodynamics and Hydrodynamics

Institute (TsAGI). Former inmates here include Yuri Orlov, Vladimir Bukovsky, Alexander Ginzburg, Anatoli Shcharansky, and Alexander Solzhenitsyn, as well as Georgii Vins the Baptist leader.

Prison is more severe than labour camp, and the inmates' health rapidly deteriorates through lack of exercise and proper food. Two regimes operate in prison, Ordinary (Obshchii), and Strict (Strogii). Under Ordinary Regime a prisoner is locked in his cell for 23 hours a day, and allowed one hour's exercise. He may write one letter a month, spend three roubles a month in the prison shop, and receive two visits a year. Under Strict Regime he is confined for twenty-three and a half hours a day, he may write one letter every two months, and spend two roubles a month in the prison shop. He may not have any visitors. No prisoner can receive parcels. Visits under Ordinary Regime may not exceed two hours and the prisoner and his visitor may not touch each other; they sit under surveillance of a guard on either side of a table divided by a wire partition. When a prisoner first arrives in prison he is put on Strict Regime for two months, or six months if he has been in prison before. For the first month he has a reduced food ration. Most cells are damp, inefficiently heated, with poor or no ventilation. Some have a toilet and sink, some just a bucket. The prisoners are usually fed through a trough in the cell door.

Avraam Shifrin spent ten years in camp imprisonment and four in exile and was eventually allowed to leave the USSR for Israel. He says that the special KGB prison Lefortovo is a most horrifying place. Prisoners are put in solitary confinement at the smallest provocation. Solitary confinement cells are kept at cool temperatures and the floors are covered with water. Cells often do not have a bed or a bench. He reports one inmate as saying: "I spent twenty-eight days in solitary confinement cell No. 3 in the basement of Lefortovo Prison. Not having a bed, I had to stand up to my ankles in water the whole time. I was given a daily ration of three hundred grams of bread, and twice a day a mug of water. After a few days in a standing position I began to fall over. Soon I found myself sitting in water and filth on the cell floor."[9] Inmates are tortured at Lefortovo by interrogation, isolation, intimidation, threats of family persecution, or by being placed in rooms with thugs already incited to attack them. "Voluntary" confessions can be extracted by such means.

The best known prison in Leningrad is right on what might be described as the tourist route. Kresty Prison is situated in Liteinyi Prospekt 4, near where you catch a trolleybus to your hotel on the outskirts of the city. Over ten thousand prisoners are kept there. Half of them have already been tried and convicted, and the rest are under investigation. Thus like Lubyanka it is in two halves. Again cell windows are sealed off with wooden boards or "muzzles". Each cell was originally built to accommodate two prisoners but now as many as eight will share the same cell. Lenin was once imprisoned here, but his windows were not "muzzled". Conditions have worsened since his day.[10] Here is Shifrin's evocation:

When I was walking from Kresty through the underground corridor to the KGB prison for interrogation, I immediately realised that I was in another place. The corridors here were wide, the guards were wearing KGB uniforms, and there was carpeting on the floors (to enable the the guards to approach the cell doors quietly and peep through the spy hole). After being shown my cell, I soon discovered that my new cell-mate and I were being listened to by microphone and even observed by camera. We decided to test this by staging a conversation about how we would use a knife we pretended to have to attack the guard. We spoke as if we had hidden it in one of the mattresses. About ten or fifteen minutes later, a group of guards burst in and handcuffed us. They cut open the mattresses but, of course, found nothing . . . We laughed.[11]

When a prisoner is sent to labour camp the type of regime is labelled Ordinary, Intensified, Strict, or Special. Each camp will operate one type of regime. Camps are surrounded by

barbed wire and walls with watchtowers and are guarded
by MVD personnel and dogs. The regimes differ in the
number of privileges allowed, the type of work done, the
quality and amount of food, and the severity of surveillance. In the four types of camp, visits diminish as the
severity increases, from five a year down to two a year.
Some visits can be private, that is a prisoner and his family
are locked up in a hut for a day, given food and left alone to
enjoy normal relations. But this will depend on the severity
of the regime. In prison no such visits are allowed, and any
meetings with relatives take place under surveillance. All
letters sent or received are subject to censorship. A prisoner
can lose any privilege for failing to fulfil his work quota, for
insubordination, or for infringing camp regulations. These
are never shown to the prisoner in full, and he is often
unaware that he has broken one until punished. Under all
regimes a prisoner is not entitled to receive any parcels until
he has completed half his labour camp sentence. Living
conditions in camp are extremely spartan. Many are situated in areas of extreme winter cold. In spite of this,
prisoners are not allowed more than one blanket and have
to wear regulation clothes in all conditions. These are black
when issued but gradually turn grey after washing. Toilets
are often situated well away from the barracks, which
makes life difficult for the elderly.

Under Ordinary and Intensified Regimes the prisoner
will work an eight-hour day without any holidays. He will
nearly always have to work overtime in order to achieve
production targets. Under Strict Regime, the work will be in
a factory or at something physically demanding such as tree
felling. Special Regime is for the "especially dangerous
persistent offender", and differs from the others in that
when not at work a prisoner may be locked up in a cell and let
out just for one hour's exercise. He will work within the con-
fines of the camp. Prisoners are woken at 6.00 a.m. each day
and may be punished for not getting out of bed immediately,
or for lying down on the bed having once got up. After
eating their morning meal, they leave for work and may not

return again until after work. Lights are put out at 10.00 p.m.
After that prisoners have to remain in their quarters.

According to Soviet Law, "every convicted person shall
have the duty of work". The commentary to the RSFSR
Criminal Code explains that "in a socialist society, where
the principle operates that "he who doesn't work doesn't
eat", labour is not only the right but also the obligation of
every citizen . . . The induction of convicted persons to
labour is necessary for rooting out their habit of a parasitic
existence of their unconscientious attitude to work".[12] In
practice work is a part of a prisoner's punishment, a fact
acknowledged by the Soviet newspaper *Kazakhstanakaya
Pravda* which said on 14 March 1973: "Work carried out by
prisoners is basically hard labour, and output norms are
maximal . . . A labour colony is not a rest home. It is a place
for serving out punishment. Here it is necessary to work.
By the sweat of one's brow". Thus camps form a part of the
Soviet economy. They have to pay their way, and expendi-
ture on prisoners' accommodation, food, and so on has to
be financed by prisoners' productivity. Many camps therefore specialise in one type of work. Convict labour is still
used in the construction industry. Inmates of the Special
Regime Camp in Mordovia worked at polishing crystal
for chandeliers. Those in a Strict Regime Camp of the
Mordovian complex of colonies produce wooden clock
frames, and do all the work from sawing the logs to
polishing the finished product. The wooden dolls known
as *matreshki* are made by prisoners. They can act as memen-
toes of Soviet prison life, as well as helping the government
with foreign currency.

Believers say that their output norms are excessively
high, and that they are difficult to achieve because of their
underlying hunger and the fact that they are not always
accustomed to that kind of work. In some cases too the
equipment is poor. The Lithuanian believer Nijole Sadunaite, who I spoke about in the last chapter, and who was
arrested in 1974 for making *samizdat* copies of the *Chronicle
of the Lithuanian Catholic Church* and was sentenced in 1975

to three years in a labour camp and three in exile for "anti-Soviet agitation and propaganda", reported from the Strict Regime women's camp in Mordovia in 1976 that the norm for sewing gloves was 70 pairs a day. She said that this was difficult to achieve because the machinery was always breaking down. As soon as she arrived at the camp her health broke down but she still had to fulfil her quota in spite of being absent for periods of the working day. She was, however, allowed to extend the day, starting work at 6.30 a.m. and ending at 10.30 p.m. in order to catch up.

Hunger is the most permanent feature of camp life. It is endemic to this system of punishment and cynically manipulated. The commentary to Article 56 of the Corrective Labour Legislation says: "Convicted persons who systematically and maliciously do not fulfil their output norms at work may be put on reduced food rations".[13] Prisoners are entirely dependent on the administration for their food, and any food obtained from other sources is confiscated.[14] According to reports from prisoners there are thirteen different diets from which the authorities can choose, depending on the prisoner's category and the type of work he is doing as well as the punishment imposed. The daily menu under Norm 1 is:

| | |
|---|---|
| Rye Bread 650 grams | Potato 450 grams |
| Wheatmeal flour 10 gr | Tomato purée 5 gr |
| Cabbage & Vegetable 200 gr | Fish 85 gr |
| Vegetable Oil 15 gr | Fat 10 gr |
| Groats 110 gr | Sugar 20 gr |
| Macaroni 20 gr | Meat 50 gr |

This totals 2,500 calories and 65 grams of protein. The World Health Organisation recommends a calorie intake of 3,100–3,900 for a man doing active work. Prisoners on strenuous work are given extra porridge, oil and sugar, but it is fair to say that in practice the shortage of food in the USSR means that most really nourishing food is stolen by the camp authorities. Meat will almost never reach a prisoner's plate. Everyone, then, will receive roughly the same diet consisting of food that no one wants to steal: rotten cabbage, rotten fish, potatoes and bread. This diet is inadequate for the kind of labour expected; has obvious consequences, swelling joints and stomach ulcers; and will aggravate any existing illness. Vladimir Bukovsky describes the effects of hunger on a prisoner having himself spent from 1972 to 1976 in Vladimir Prison and Perm camps.

I can't say prison hunger was particularly agonising – it wasn't a biting hunger but, rather, a prolonged process of chronic undernourishment. You very quickly stopped feeling it badly and were left with a kind of gnawing pain, rather like a quietly throbbing toothache. You even lost awareness that it was hunger, and only after several months did you notice that it hurt to sit on a wooden bench, and at night, no matter which way you turned, something hard seem to be pressing into you or against you – you would get up several times in the night and shake the mattress, toss and turn from side to side, and still it hurt. Only then did you realise that your bones were sticking out. By then you didn't care any longer. Nevertheless, you didn't get out of your bunk too quickly in the mornings, otherwise your head would spin.[15]

In spite of their constant undernourishment, believers often resort to hunger strikes as a means of protest. This is very clearly and movingly shown in the *samizdat* document smuggled out of the Women's Camp in Mordovia, which tells of the unique resistance by Christian prisoners to the repression and arbitrary violence of the camp authorities. The report was compiled in late 1984 and indicates that "places of confinement" are becoming stricter and more inhumane. In August Natalya Lazareva and Tatyana Osipova were taken into solitary confinement for refusing to wear their identification tags and for absenting themselves from work. Osipova got ten days, Lazareva thirteen. The others then declared a strike in sympathy:

On the fifth day of our hunger strike, when we were all very weak, Vladimirova (she never participates in our activities) began to threaten us with physical reprisals. Since then we have periodically heard that "they'll turn us into a pile of corpses" and have received individual murder threats . . . On the seventh day of our hunger strike Tatyana Velikanova, Raisa Rudenko and Irina Ratushinskaya were "isolated" in the infirmary. On the eighth day they were fed by force. Velikanova and Ratushinskaya resisted and were handcuffed and forced by six men. In the course of this procedure they banged Ratushinskaya's head against a trestle-bed and poured liquid down her throat while she was unconscious. Velikanova revived her in the cell in the psychiatric section where they were locked up after the feeding. The windowless cell is never aired, and they were not taken out for exercise. They spent five days under these conditions. Judging from the after effects of the feeding procedure (enlarged pupils, nausea, vertigo, and a headache which persists to this day), Ratushinskaya suffered concussion, but the doctor did not examine her, although therapist Vera Aleksandrovna Volkova took part in the procedure and must have seen what happened. The story became the talk of the infirmary, and it was decided to stop force feeding Velikanova and Ratushinskaya".[16]

It is amazing how human beings can react under such dehumanising and brutalising conditions. The following is taken from a letter written from prison by the Russian Orthodox believer Alexander Ogorodnikov to his parents, which was received by Keston College at the beginning of 1982:

How can I express the love that fills my heart to overflowing and gives breath into my lungs? I love you very much, and that love has acquired a tenderness I have never experienced before and which has strengthened behind these bare and terrifying walls . . . My tongue cannot find sufficient words to express all that I feel and cannot express my thoughts and my prayers for you . . . How rarely your letters reach me! The head of the operations sector in the camp has told me that the packet of medicines that you sent me has been returned to you, so it is not just letters but essential medicines that don't get through. I know from the "mail confiscation notice" that you are living in Redkino. When I am not given your letters I am occasionally shown (but not always, because at times the KGB does not even tell me that a letter has arrived) a "Notice of Confiscation" on which the name and address of the sender is entered. I was also informed of your move by the chekists[17] from Kalinin – head of investigation section G. P. Petrov and the head of operations, a fellow with sharp challenging eyes and a crooked smile. They came here on 27 October 1981 and tried, once again, to persuade me to recant. My dear ones, there is so much I have to say to you – pray God this letter reaches you. On 9 October I was put in the punishment cell where the regime is harsher than prison. Rations are minimal, but I am refusing them.[18]

Ogorodnikov had been on hunger strike since 28 October 1981, demanding the return of his Bible and prayerbook, to see a priest, to receive religious literature, to subscribe to religious periodicals published in the USSR, to enrol as a correspondence student in the theological academy, to receive visits from his parents and to register his marriage with Yelena. He was also protesting about the lack of light in his cell. It was switched off from 10.00 a.m. until 4.00 p.m. and used to be switched off even earlier, so that he spent literally the whole day in semi-darkness.

Internal exile can be given as a sentence in itself, or in addition to a term in prison or labour camp. The prisoner will be transported under conditions of detention to the area of exile, where he is handed over to the local authorities. They assign him to a town or village where he has to live and is given a job. This will tend to be the lowest paid and most difficult available. He is not subject to any other conditions, except that he must report to the local authorities at regular intervals of about a week or fortnight. Representatives of the authorities may call on him at any time of day or night to check that he is still there, or to search the house. He can receive as many visitors and letters as he likes and these are not censored. A surprising number do get through, even from abroad. Any relative may come and live with the exile, but he is confined to that place and cannot leave the immediate district. Many families, however, do not join their loved ones in exile because they run the risk of losing their residence permit if their permanent home is in one of the major cities. Local authorities may give the exile permission to visit a dying relative, for example, but are under no obligation to do so.

A friend has described the situation of Zoya Krakhmalni-kova in exile in the Altai mountains near the Chinese border. She was the compiler of *Nadezhda* (Hope) and was sentenced to one year imprisonment and five in exile in 1983:

> The thin air of the mountains makes breathing difficult and the temperatures fall to 30 or 40 degrees below zero. She is suffering from poor circulation, anaemia caused by narrowing of the arteries, constant pains in the legs and stomach. It is impossible to get dental treatment anywhere. Zoya is living in the barracks on the edge of the village. Water has to be carried from a tap some distance away. Even getting firewood is no easy matter, and with those frosts you need it! Food supplies are poor and there are not vegetables at all. Those responsible for her supervision are constantly watching her. In recent months the "visits" from the authorities have become more frequent, but of course not with the intention of helping a woman alone in a strange place. In fact one should rather fear the contrary. The fear is confirmed by the following incident: at the end of last year the local authorities unexpectedly gave permission for Zoya to go to Moscow for necessary medical tests. Such periods of "leave" from exile are exceptionally rarely granted. And so it was this time: the permission was withdrawn . . . Zoya has plenty of time for reflection and prayer, for which there is not always time in the hectic life of Moscow. She accepts everything as the will of God, thanks him for his mercy and walks her path quietly, humbly and prayerfully, as a Christian should, who is bearing the cross of Christ.[19]

It might be thought there is still something nineteenth century about "internal exile" in the USSR. However, there is no church where Zoya Krakhmalnikova is forced to live. The nearest are many kilometres away in Biisk and Barnaul; as an exile, she is not allowed to go.

Perhaps the worst form of imprisonment is forcible confinement in a psychiatric hospital. Psychiatry has always been open to abuse. The first recorded case of psychiatric abuse in Russia is thought to be the detention of Pyotr Chaadayev, the Catholic philosopher, by Tsar Nicholas 1 in 1836. He was declared to be "deranged and insane" and was put away for criticising the Tsar's government. This was, however, an isolated event and not part of usual state policy. It is well known that there was a good deal of abuse of psychiatry in the Stalin period as there was in other fields. His successor Khrushchev wanted to clean up Russia's image in the free world. There is, however, little evidence to show that fewer dissidents were confined to psychiatric hospitals during the 1960s and 1970s. Indeed, few people outside Russia knew much about what was going on until after 1968.

There are two types of psychiatric hospital. The first is an Ordinary Psychiatric Hospital (OPH). These are administered by the Ministry of Health, and the police may bring individuals for treatment whom they accuse of peculiar behaviour. These may be described as short stay hospitals. People can be sent in for a matter of days or weeks, and they are used as a method of getting dissidents off the streets during the visits of foreign leaders or other important events. This was widely done during the 1980 Olympics. However, some dissidents are confined to an OPH for years.

The second type of hospital is called a Special Psychiatric Hospital (SPH), and confinement to one of these is a very different story. Many believers are charged under Article 70 of the RSFSR Criminal Code (see chapter 5), and investigation can be followed by clinical examination by a psychiatric commission who have the power to decide whether or not a person is mentally responsible. If they decide that he is not, a believer is not allowed to attend his own trial, and the courts do their best to keep out family and friends as well. Thus the trial becomes a formality. Relatives can appeal after the believer is sentenced to psychiatric hospital, but the accused himself has no right of appeal on the grounds of his own mental incompetence.

The type of hospital to which he is committed has enormous bearing upon what happens to the believer. Ordinary Psychiatric Hospitals are usually situated in towns and have an out-patients department, and one would normally be confined to the nearest OPH, and therefore retain some contact with the outside world. Whereas Special Psychiatric Hospitals are often run as a part of the prison system by the MVD and prisoners may be sent anywhere in the USSR. Here a believer may be surrounded by patients with severe mental illnesses; many of them will have committed violent crimes such as rape, assault, and murder. The organisation of SPH is also quite different from an OPH. The doctors are not in full control of the patients and are subject to the hospital director, who is not a psychiatrist. The nurses are guards, and they control the orderlies, who are known to be criminals serving sentences and easily corrupted. Nurses and medical staff are subject to the security demands of the institution, and find it difficult to act humanely towards patients even if they wished to do so. All of which makes it unlikely that committal to an SPH will result in a cure. This can be seen through the eyes of a former inmate of a Special Psychiatric Hospital, Vladimir Bukovsky:

In fact Leningrad Special Hospital was just an ordinary prison with detention cells, bars on the windows, barbed wire, a high wall, armed guards, and where the "patients" had restricted rights to correspondence and food parcels. (Theoretically the guards weren't supposed to shoot at a mental patient trying to escape. But how were they to tell a patient from one of the crooks working as orderlies? Naturally, the safest thing was to shoot, and that had already happened on some occasions). Added to all the usual prison worries were the worries specific to psychiatric detention – indefinite confinement, compulsory treatment, beatings and a total lack of rights. There was also no one to complain to, for every complaint got lodged in your case history as yet one more proof of your insanity. None of us was sure if he would ever leave there alive. Some of our fellows were already in trouble – they had had injections and others were getting pills.

It is no simple matter to prove that you are sane, or at least on the road to recovery. What doctor wants to overturn his colleagues' diagnoses or take responsibility for discharging you? It is far easier to go along with things.

It was well known that although, formally speaking, our detention was supposed to be indefinite, in practice murderers were usually held for five or six years and our sort for two or three – that is, if you submitted completely, were involved in no conflicts and had no bad reports on your observation record.[20]

Dissenters of every kind committed to SPH share one basic feature – they have deviated from social conventions and norms laid down by the State. They can be classified as follows: human rights activists, nationalists, would-be emigrants, religious believers, and people inconvenient to the authorities. Here are two examples of different types of people detained in SPHs. The first is a human rights activist who has since become a Christian; the second was sentenced whilst already a believer.

Viktor Davydov was born in 1956 in the Volga City of Kuibyshev and at the time of his arrest was a law student. He was committed for his part in human rights activities and for writing *samizdat* articles on the Stalin period and the failings of the Soviet system. He was subject to psychiatric examination from 1979, and in October of that year sought an independent examination by Dr Alexander Voloshanovich, who was then consultant to the Moscow Working Commission to Investigate the Use of Psychiatry for Political Purposes. Voloshanovich concluded that Davydov was in no way schizophrenic and was "fully responsible for his actions". A month later he was arrested and charged under Article 70 with "anti-Soviet agitation and propaganda". He was then examined by a psychiatric commission, who found him to be responsible, but he was nonetheless transferred to the notorious Serbsky Institute. Here in mid-1980 he was diagnosed as a mild schizophrenic and judged not responsible. At his trial the court accepted the Serbsky report alone, saying: "In view of the great social danger he represents he needs to undergo compulsory treatment in a psychiatric hospital of special type".[21] After a spell in Kazan SPH Davydov was sent to Blagoveshchensk SPH near the Chinese border, 4,500 kilometres from his wife and friends. In a statement made to the 1985 Sakharov Hearing he described in graphic terms what it is like for a sane man to be detained in a psychiatric hospital. He said:

Anyone who is interested will have already heard about the abuse of psychiatry in the Soviet Union. I had also heard about it before my arrest, but when I found myself in a Special Psychiatric Hospital then I understood that all the talk up to that time was like a lie. The truth was ten times worse, and what I endured in the first few days there was a tremendous shock for me personally. It destroyed all my notions of humanitarism, justice, and of the high name of the human being. I understood that people were being turned into consciousless creatures. This was not second-hand, but my own personal experience.

The first thing that happened was that I was given two injections for refusing to have my hair cut and my beard shaved. For almost three days I was in a state of complete irresponsibility verging on the insane. I did not know the difference between being awake and asleep, and could not distinguish between reality and dream. This was accompanied by an inability to control my own body and by appalling physical pain. They stopped the injections, but started giving me pills. To begin with nothing much happened. But a few hours later I began to be unable to control my body. It became impossible to sit or lie down. You had to keep moving. I was completely unable to order my body to do anything – still less control my thoughts. In other words you had to work hard to prevent everything from turning into a flow of unconsciousness. I felt that I was being turned into an inhuman creature, incapable of thought, who could only think of food and sleep and beyond that nothing. I was turned by those persecutors into a mere animal, whose thoughts are of no interest to anyone. This stage passed and gave way to total apathy, and a lack of interest in anything.[22]

Various believers have been detained in Special Psychiatric Hospitals simply because they have held fast to their right under the Soviet Constitution freely to practise their religion. Amnesty International estimate that about 15% of the 210 cases examined by them are religious believers. One such person is Vladimir Khailo, a Baptist who was arrested in September 1980 and sentenced to Dnepropetrovsk SPH. In this letter by his wife Mariya she describes the hospital:

Many think that this is simply a hospital. In fact it is a closed prison patrolled by guards. All the so-called medical workers wear military uniform under their white overalls. My husband is strictly guarded. He wears prison clothing, all black, and his hair has been cropped. He is taken for a walk for one hour each day. The windows of the buildings are fitted with iron bars and through them neither earth nor sky is visible, only the roofs of other buildings. As soon as he was taken there they put him in a room where there were 27 other people. It was very crowded. They had to climb over each other to get to their beds. Immediately the authorities started to give out tablets so that the prisoners slept day and night. If anyone did not go to sleep he was given an extra dose. The food is poor.

A month after he was taken there I was allowed to visit him. When I arrived I could not recognise him. His skin had become quite dark as a result of the tablets he had had to take. He had become unrecognisable and suddenly very weak. After the visit he had two months of quarantine and in the course of these two months they destroyed his health. They gave him 30 tablets of haloperidol in one dose after which he swelled up completely and his heart started to fail. His blood pressure rose, his vision deteriorated and he lost consciousness. I sent telegrams to the Presidium and to Brezhnev, but did not receive any reply. They then changed the haloperidol and started to give him injections. They told him that they were treating his heart condition and gave him aminazin tablets. They then changed from aminazin and prescribed stilazin. They had reduced him to such a state that he constantly had pains in his heart. His hands refused to function and he cannot lift his right arm. I appealed to the Ministry of Health, but have not received any reply. They then changed from stilazin and now they are giving him triftazin. My husband said that after he has been given these tablets he feels everything in his body contract – his eyes twitch and his mouth twists to one side.[23]

These two accounts, supported by others not mentioned in this book, show how the authorities in both types of psychiatric hospital in the Soviet Union often administer drugs indiscriminately and routinely to patients without attention to size of dosage, or possible side effects. These drugs are sometimes given on arrival at the psychiatric hospital without the patient even being diagnosed by a psychiatrist.

World attention has been focussed on the misuse of psychiatric hospitals in the USSR since the beginning of the human rights movement in the mid-1960s. In 1971 Vladimir Bukovksy compiled a 150-page documentary and detailed case study of abuses. He sent it to the West for study by psychiatrists. In 1973 Andrei Sakharov appealed for Western action against the political misuse of psychiatry in the Soviet Union. That year the Soviets hosted the World Psychiatric Association (WPA) and some Western psychiatrists visited the Serbsky Institute. The Soviets hoped to convince the West that any criticism was groundless. They failed to do so. Against this background, in August 1977 at the sixth World Congress of the WPA in Honolulu a resolution was passed condemning Soviet practices in this field. This culminated in the resignation of the Soviet Psychiatric Society from the WPA in January 1983. Since then there has been some improvement in Soviet practices and a drop in the number of dissenters subjected to Special Psychiatric Hospitals. This is good news but Viktor Davydov says that there are still numbers of dissenters of all sorts in these hospitals, and that the misuse of psychiatric medicine in the USSR must remain on the international agenda. He says: "It is a blight upon civilisation committed by people whose job it is to bring joy to patients. Instead they are tormenting them and depriving them of their lives. This abuse hasn't stopped".[24]

The truth of that statement can be seen from the case of the Catholic believer Sandr Riga, who was only recently charged with "setting up an unregistered religious group of Christian ecumenists and editing a religious *samizdat* journal *Prizyv* [The Call]". A medical examination under the supervision of Professor Snezhnevsky found him psychiatrically abnormal, the diagnosis being "latent creeping schizophrenia". At the closed trial neither his family nor Riga himself were present, he was sentenced to compulsory psychiatric treatment. Riga himself only learned of the sentence from his mother when she visited him. The writer of the report states that his case is: "absolutely illegal even according to the norms of Soviet judicial practice".[25]

# 8

# International Law

Up to this point we have been looking at the domestic laws of the USSR and their application to believers, and now need to examine these in the international context. For in reality the world constitutes a single society and that society needs laws of its own. Thus for many centuries there has been a system of International Law designed to regulate the relationship between sovereign states. For most of these centuries International Law took little account of national laws. Indeed the whole concept of national sovereignty meant that all important matters were the exclusive province of each sovereign state and not the concern of any other state or of International Law. International Law therefore dealt with matters like war and peace between sovereign nations, diplomatic relations, and international shipping on the high seas. An individual was protected by the domestic laws of his own country and could never be the subject of International Law in the sense of having any rights which would be recognised. The way in which a state treated its own citizens was regarded as entirely its personal concern.

This doctrine held sway until well into the present century and was successfully quoted by a series of tyrants who, if protests were made against their actions, replied that such protests were an "illegitimate interference in the internal affairs of a sovereign state". Ironically it was Hitler and Stalin who toppled that doctrine. The atrocities which they perpetuated against millions of their citizens truly shocked the conscience of mankind, and helped precipitate a world war of unprecedented ferocity. But the point is that what Hitler did to the Jews, gypsies, and other minorities was done with full domestic legality in accordance with the Nuremberg Laws.[1] He acted under the constitutionally elected legislature of a sovereign German State. In other words his actions did not contravene national law. Similarly Stalin's persecution of the *kulaks* could be justified by the same legal formula. To have made a protest in either case would have brought forth the reply: "you are interfering in the internal affairs of a sovereign state". Clearly the conscience of mankind could not longer tolerate such a state of affairs, in which international law had to accept the *status quo* because it was beyond its control. Something had to be done to ensure that in future mere national legality was not enough to validate the murder of one's own people. Somehow an international standard of legitimacy had to be installed by which one could assess the conduct of a national government, not only in its external affairs, but in its domestic ones. In the last two decades a code called Human Rights Law has been accepted as part of the world's international legal order.

This law is made up of the United Nations Charter, the Universal Declaration of Human Rights, and the twin International Covenants – the International Covenant on Civil and Political Rights, and the International Covenant on Economic, Social and Cultural Rights. The effect of all this on International Law was well expressed by Professor H. Lauterpacht: "the individual has acquired a status and a stature which has transformed him from an object of international compassion into a subject of international right".[2] In installing this new code of International Law the world's nations have drawn on the many precedents in their own legal systems: struggles for individual liberty, autonomy, equality before the law, freedom from torture and slavery, freedom of conscience and speech. Many other civil liberties and rights have been fought for and won in many countries over the centuries. There has been a steady evolution from the English Magna Carta of 1215 to the United States' Bill of Rights of 1791. Their statements are in a sense universal, and their influence has spread into the international community. However, until recently these human rights were not determined by the content of an international code. Now any violation of that code becomes a matter of legitimate concern for all other nations and their peoples. So their protests can no longer be dismissed as "an illegitimate interference in the internal affairs of a sovereign state".

If world opinion protests about the way believers are held in labour camps in the USSR, then, it is not because it prefers a capitalist system to a socialist one. It is not because the protesters are of one religion or another, or humanists or atheists, or because they are brought up in a liberal tradition. It is because the Soviet Union was one of the original signatories to the Charter of the United Nations. She took a full part in drafting the twin covenants, which form the main components of the new global code, namely the International Covenant on Civil and Political Rights, and the International Covenant on Economic, Social and Cultural Rights. She was a party to their adoption in 1966, and signed them both on 18 March 1968. She ratified them both on 16 October 1973, thus becoming legally bound by them when they entered into force in 1976. Indeed it was the Soviet Union's close ally Czechoslovakia who deposited the 35th instrument of ratification which finally brought them into force.

At this point it is worth noticing the difference between the signature and ratification of a treaty. Most written documents come into force when the two parties have signed them. In the past, however, this was not often the case with treaties since it was only after the plenipotentiary had returned to his own court that it was possible for the sovereign to examine the text and decide whether or not he wished to be bound by it. Signature then tended to indicate adoption of the text as authentic, and a further step called ratification, that is acceptance or approval, was necessary before the treaty could become binding. Accordingly, with the USSR's *ratification* of these covenants the treatment of any Soviet citizen by the authorities of the Soviet Union is today a matter of international law. And this can be objectively assessed by interpreting and applying provisions of the UN Charter, the Universal Declaration of Human Rights, and two covenants, independently of any personal views one may hold on the morality, politics, economics, ideology or anything else of the USSR.

The Human Rights instruments agreed to under international law may be briefly summarised as follows:

1. **The United Nations Charter (UNCH).** The United Nations are an inter-governmental organisation, whose constituent instrument is its Charter, signed in San Francisco on 26 June 1945. Article 1 includes among its purposes, "to achieve international cooperation . . . in promoting and encouraging respect for human rights and for fundamental freedoms for all".

   Articles 55 and 56 record the "pledge" of the UN member states to take joint or separate action to achieve "universal respect for, and observance, of, human rights and fundamental freedoms for all". UNCH contains no definition or catalogue of human rights and fundamental freedoms. But that omission cannot deprive the obligation of all meaning. Besides, it has since been made good by the adoption of the Universal Declaration of Human Rights. Today it is almost universally agreed that the UNCH obligation is binding in international law on all UN members, and is direct and unqualified.

2. **The Universal Declaration of Human Rights (UDHR).** The first catalogue of human rights and fundamental freedoms enumerated by the UN was the UDHR, which was a declaration of the UN General Assembly adopted in Paris on 10 December 1948. At that time the UN had 56 members, 46 voted in favour, none against, and eight abstained. They were Belorussia, Czechoslovakia, Poland, the Ukraine, the USSR, Yugoslavia, Saudi

Arabia, and South Africa. The catalogue of human rights set out in UDHR contains 28 Articles, followed by a further article on duties and limitations, and another on abuse.

The actual judicial status of UDHR remains a matter of some controversy. It is plain from the debates in the United Nations General Assembly in 1948 that it was not by itself intended to create binding obligations in international law for the UN's member states. Indeed, the preamble ends with the following words: "Now, therefore, the General Assembly proclaims this Universal Declaration of Human Rights as a common standard of achievement for all peoples and all nations, to the end that every individual and every organ of society, keeping this Declaration in mind, shall strive by teaching and education to promote respect for these rights and freedoms and by progressive measures, national and international, to secure their universal and effective recognition and observance, both among the peoples of member states themselves and among the peoples of territories under their jurisdiction".

Some commentators say that UDHR cannot itself create binding obligations, yet many will accept that it does, not because it has become a part of customary international law, but because they have expressly accepted their obligations. Thus the USSR for example is bound by UDHR because Articles 55 and 56 UDHR create a legal obligation called the "pledge" for all the UN member states to take action and have respect for human rights and fundamental freedoms. UNCH does not enumerate these rights and freedoms, but UDHR does. The preamble to UDHR says: "Member states have pledged themselves to achieve . . . the promotion of universal respect for and observation of human rights and fundamental freedoms".[3]

3. **The International Covenant on Civil and Political Rights (ICPR).** At the same time and on the assumption that UDHR would not impose sufficiently binding

obligations, the UN Commission on Human Rights drafted the covenants on human rights designed to become legally binding on UN member states. That work began in 1947 and was completed in 1954, when the two covenants were presented to the UN General Assembly. They were the ICPR and ICES. They were adopted by the UNGA in 1966, and came into force on 23 March 1976. They have been signed and ratified by the USSR.

ICPR contains 27 Articles defining in much greater detail than the UDHR a variety of rights and freedoms, and imposing in Article 2 an absolute and immediate obligation on each of the state parties to "respect and ensure" these rights "to all individuals within its territories and subject to its jurisdiction". The instrument also establishes a human rights committee having competence in three matters. First, to comment on reports to be submitted by the state parties on the measures they have adopted to comply with their obligations under the covenant. Second, to investigate complaints of failures by other states to fulfil their obligations under the covenant. Third, to investigate complaints from victims of such failures. Since 1976 the Human Rights Commission has been very active and examined a considerable number of complaints.

4. **The International Covenant on Economic Social and Cultural Rights (ICES).** This instrument drafted in parallel with ICPR has followed the same history. It was presented to the UNGA in 1954, adopted in 1966, and entered into force on 3 January 1976. Again, it has been signed and ratified by the USSR. The covenant contains 15 Articles defining in detail a set of rights largely derived from the UDHR. But in this instance the obligations assumed by state parties in Article 2 are qualified; unlike ICPR each one only "undertakes to take steps . . . to the maximum of its available resources . . . with a view to achieving progressively the full realisation of the rights recognised . . . by all appropriate means". ICES

has no provision for interpreting and applying the covenant. Instead it provides a reporting procedure through the UN Secretary General to the UN Economic and Social Council who may transmit reports to the Commission on Human Rights.

Let us look at some of the more essential points in the code itself. This is by no means a complete list, but I have chosen Articles which cover the violations described in the previous chapters, and listed them under the following points:

**1. The right to life, liberty and security of person** The UN Charter places great emphasis on the quality of life, trying to ensure that, in the words of Article 3 of the Universal Declaration of Human Rights, "everyone has the right to life, liberty and security of person". This is also reflected in the ICPR Article 9(1): "Everyone has the right to liberty and security of person. No one shall be deprived of his liberty except on such grounds and in accordance with such procedures as are established by law". And on arrest a prisoner must be brought "promptly" to trial.

Thus in the case of the detention in Gorki of Academician Andrei Sakharov, according to international agreement it is quite illegal to force him to leave Moscow against his will: this constitutes a violation under international law. Sakharov has not been accused of any crime, let alone convicted. His wife, Yelena Bonner, has been sentenced to exile for "anti-Soviet slander", but she was sentenced in Gorki to be exiled to Gorki! Before she was sentenced she was free to travel to Moscow. However, Sakharov himself is not guilty of any breach of administrative regulations and the steps taken against him have not been sanctioned by any court. In other words he has been sent away from Moscow against his will and detained in Gorki in direct contravention of International Laws signed and ratified by the Soviet Government.

**2. The right to be treated with humanity and respect**
Article 5 of the UDHR and Article 7 of the ICPR both declare that "no one shall be subject to torture or to cruel, inhuman, or degrading treatment or punishment". ICPR Article 10(1) adds that "All persons deprived of their liberty shall be treated with humanity and with respect for the inherent dignity of the human person". Torture may be defined as "the deliberate and wanton infliction of severe pain or suffering". This certainly happens in numerous instances in the labour camps of the USSR, and has been amply described in the foregoing chapters. The torturer in the broad sense has disappeared, but has been replaced by a more subtle and ingenious system.

**3. The right to liberty of movement**   The UDHR and ICPR state in Articles 9 and 12 respectively under Freedom of Movement that "Everyone lawfully within the territory of a state shall . . . have the right to liberty of movement and freedom to choose his residence". He shall also be free to leave his country. This is not subject to any restrictions except "those necessary to protect national security and public order". The UDHR states that "no one shall be subject to arbitrary exile". However, clearly these articles are quite contrary to the spirit of Marxism with its emphasis on a planned economy. We have already seen how there is gross disregard for them in the USSR.

**4. The prohibition of slavery, servitude and forced labour**
Forced labour is defined by the International Labour Organisation as "all work of service which is extracted from any person under menace or any penalty, and for which that person has not offered himself voluntarily". This is forbidden by the UDHR Article 4 and by Article 8 of the ICPR. Prohibition is as absolute and unqualified as with torture, but with three exceptions. These are work forming a part of a prison sentence, military service, and service performed in a national emergency.

**5. The right to freedom of thought, conscience and religion**   UDHR Article 18 and ICPR Article 18 both declare on thought, conscience and religion: "Everyone has the right to freedom of thought, conscience and religion; this right includes freedom to change his religion or belief, and freedom, either alone or in community with others and in public or private, to manifest his religious belief in teaching, practice, worship and observance". The ICPR Covenant adds in Article 20 (2): "Any advocacy of . . . religious hatred that constitutes incitement to discrimination, hostility or violence shall be prohibited by law". Article 27 says that where a religious minority exists its members "shall not be denied the right, in community with other members of the group, to profess and practise their own religion".

**6.** This elaborates the last point: "Everyone has a right to freedom of opinion and expression; this right includes freedom to hold opinions without interference and to seek, receive and impart information and ideas through any media and regardless of frontiers". (UDHR Article 19). This wording is followed closely in ICPR Article 19 as well, which adds that this carries special respect for the rights or reputation of others and protection of national security and public order.

**7. Freedom of Association**   UDHR Article 20(1) says that "Everyone has the right to freedom of association" and (2) that "No one may be compelled to belong to any association". These points are reflected in ICPR Article 22 which contains two important statements. First people may join together in associations in order to attain various ends, (for example this could include non-registered Baptists and Pentecostals). And second that no one may be compelled to belong to an association, (recalling the pressures in the Soviet Union on young people to join the Pioneers and Komsomol).[4]

In the last analysis it needs to be said that all human rights exist for the benefit of individuals or groups who are weak, and who need protection from oppression, persecution, exploitation and deprivation by those who are strong. If their weakness comes from some difference which distinguishes them from the majority they will be seen as a minority regardless of how many there are. And so in a way all human rights exist for the protection of minorities.

This is all very well but is it really possible to enforce these international laws? It is obvious that there have been many violations of them in the USSR alone. Is there indeed any point in having a law at all unless there is the clear ability to enforce it?

This is the difficulty. Ideally, individual nations will anchor human rights laws into their own constitutions, and frame laws in their country which may militate against themselves. For example, if a state signs a declaration against torture it must make sure that torture is not inflicted by its police, prisons and places of detention, and punish officials who break the law. In other words the state must introduce laws to defend the individual against torture. States differ in good faith and the way they keep international obligations on human rights. Some countries will not ratify a treaty until they have passed domestic laws to support it. Others will ratify the treaty and do little to carry out their legal obligations. A human rights treaty is not like a commercial agreement, because there is no immediate sanction on failure to carry out the terms. In human rights if you do not carry out the terms little, it seems, can be done by the UN or international pressure.

Why do countries enter into these agreements? Some do it for good reasons, others because they want to look like a humanitarian state in the eyes of the world, or simply to improve their image abroad. But why do governments not take more action to see that these agreements are carried out? The fact is that each nation's foreign policy is chiefly concerned with its own interests, and so it may well not be to their advantage to demonstrate against the human rights record of another state. The feeling still lingers that you should not interfere in the internal affairs of another country. On the other hand, now that human rights are a matter of international law it should be different. There are tribunals to judge such matters, as was done with the Greek Colonels in December 1969. In conclusion it has to be admitted that international law has been unable to do much for dissenters of various kinds in the Soviet Union. How long have different organisations been trying to get the release of Andrei Sakharov from illegal exile in Gorki? This is why great pressure needs to come from non-government sources like the Red Cross, Amnesty International, the World Council of Churches, the International Commission of Jurists, as well as from individuals.

One further move in the direction of an internationally accepted code of human rights needs to be looked at, and one which is more often quoted than all the others, namely the Helsinki Final Act. From July 1973 to July 1975 an inter-government conference on security and co-operation in Europe met in Helsinki and Geneva in order to negotiate an accord designed to reflect the policy of détente. That is, to formalise peaceful relations in Europe between the nations of East and West following the Second World War, which had never been terminated by a comprehensive peace treaty. Thirty-five nations took part, and the negotiations culminated in the Final Act signed in Helsinki on 1 August 1975. Under Principle 7 "the participating states will have respect for human rights and fundamental freedoms, including freedom of thought, conscience, religion or belief, for all without distinction as to race, sex, language or religion". It was also agreed that "participating states will recognise and respect the freedom of the individual to profess and practise, alone or in community with others, religion or belief acting in accordance with the dictates of his own conscience".

The Helsinki Final Act declares that it is not "eligible for registration under Article 102 of the Charter of the United

Nations". Accordingly, it imposes no binding obligations under international law and so has no formal legal effect. Interestingly, the ICPR and ICES did not come into force until seven months after the Helsinki Final Act was adopted and signed. But as I mentioned earlier, its political impact has been far greater than the binding treaties themselves, chiefly because each of the participating states undertook to publish the text to its own people and make it as widely known as possible. This was also done in the USSR and various spontaneous unofficial citizens' groups immediately began gathering information about human rights violations.

In fact the human rights movement in the USSR had begun in the mid-1960s. The birthday of the movement is generally considered to be 5 December 1965, when the first demonstration using human rights slogans took place on Pushkin Square, Moscow. The movement was born of the experience of people who lived in conditions of lawlessness, cruelty, and assault on the personality. They renounced the use of force and violence. As human rights activist Andrei Amalrik put it: "the dissidents accomplished something that was simple to the point of genius; in an unfree country they behaved like free men, thereby changing the moral atmosphere and the nation's governing traditions".[5] The chief aim of the movement was to exercise civil rights guaranteed under the Constitution: freedom of speech and of the press, the right to public demonstration and free association. A Committee for Human Rights in the USSR was formed in Moscow in November 1970. It acquired worldwide recognition in 1975 when Andrei Sakharov was awarded the Nobel Peace Prize. For as one of the founding members he represented the spirit of the whole movement: self-sacrifice, a willingness to help persons illegally persecuted whether or not they held the same convictions, intellectual tolerance, and an unwavering insistence on the rights and dignity of the individual.

The signatories to the Helsinki Final Act agreed to two important points. First to recognise the permanence of the post-war frontiers in Europe. This was especially important to the Soviet Union, who wanted international acceptance of her post-1945 boundaries. Second, in exchange for this went a promise to respect human rights. However, the USSR could claim, and has claimed, that this second point constitutes a violation of the first – for this in effect amounts to an "interference in the internal affairs of a sovereign state".

This division of thought was especially illustrated by the attitude of the two Germanies. West Germany (FRG) claimed that Helsinki intended "to create a state of peace in Europe in which the German Nation will regain its unity through self-determination". East Germany (GDR) argued that inviolability of frontiers was the "decisive point" in the Helsinki agreement and that the Final Act would not allow for peaceful change of borders. Thus the Final Act was something of a hybrid document which reflected unresolved tensions between East and West.[6]

The Helsinki Declaration is not a formal treaty and so does not endow the Soviet position in Eastern Europe with the *de jure* legitimacy that Moscow hoped for. Yet the West did acknowledge the *de facto* situation, thus making East–West confrontation in Europe more remote than it had been since the Berlin crisis of 1961.

Two views may be taken of the Soviet dominance of Eastern Europe. The first is exemplified by Helmut Sonnenfeldt, who suggested that states within the Soviet sphere should be ready to accept their geographical proximity to the USSR, a fact that cannot be changed, and that this was unlikely to alter in the foreseeable future. Consequently, he said, there was need for an "organic relationship" between the USSR and the rest of Eastern Europe. This view poses great problems both for the USA, who do not want to accept Eastern Europe's subservience to the Soviet Union as a permanent feature, and West Germany, who have given up reunification in the short term but not permanently. The second view was put by George Schultz at the opening of the Stockholm Conference in January 1984, when he said: "the United States does not recognise the legitimacy of the artificially imposed division of Europe. This division is the essence of Europe's security and human rights problem, and we all know it".[7]

This latter view has given enormous encouragement to dissenters in the Soviet Union and Eastern Europe. The Carter Administration was extremely forceful in exerting pressure on Moscow to observe the provisions of the Helsinki declaration. The continuing review process embodied in the conferences at Belgrade and Madrid, and the establishing of monitoring agencies and groups in the USA and Western Europe, have helped to keep attention focused on questions of Soviet compliance. Yet there has been a price. The injection of the human rights issue into Soviet–US relations by Senator Henry Jackson and then by President Carter contributed to the souring of superpower relations in the middle and late 1970s. Furthermore, there is the danger that if unrest is encouraged in Eastern Europe the result will be more Soviet repression which the West will be unwilling or unable to resist. The grand result could be for the West to score on points in the propaganda battle, but to achieve little concrete help for dissidents.

The commonly held view at the time was that the humanitarian articles of the Final Act were little more than a gesture by the Soviet Government in deference to public opinion in the democratic countries. Be that as it may, Soviet citizens were stunned by the publication of the complete text of the Final Act. It was the first most of them knew of any international obligations signed by their government in the human rights field. Yuri Orlov saw in this a possible way of bringing Soviet citizens together with their government and society. He argued that this was the only way to liberalise the regime and to resolve the moral crisis in the USSR. He had attempted something of the sort in 1956 and had been exiled to Armenia for 15 years. In 1971 he returned to Moscow and sent a letter to Brezhnev asking the Soviet leaders to listen to their own citizens. He also knew that writers, scientists, and religious organisations in the West were becoming interested in the human rights issue in the USSR. But no government had as yet appealed directly to the Soviet leaders demanding that they observe their own signed international agreements on human rights. The Governments of the democratic countries did not show equal interest in the status of human rights in the USSR. Not once had any international organisation tried to verify whether the Soviet Union was fulfilling its obligations in international law in the context of the work of the UN Human Rights Commission.

Orlov saw an opportunity of using the Final Act to spur the West into a mediating role. The Act allows for this as a way of preserving peace, which is one of its major aims. Thus freedom of information ceases to be just the concern of individual governments but of everyone, and in the case of violations of humanitarian articles it is normal for other partners to apply pressure on the offender. Orlov understood that the rights laid out in the articles were a minimum international standard for countries who had signed the Helsinki accords. Added to this, the Final Act contains an appeal to the citizens of signatory countries to assist their governments in observing the accords, because mere government efforts to preserve peace might well prove inadequate. Thus the Moscow Helsinki Watch Group was formed in May 1976 to monitor violations of human rights. It served to inform the public and government about the Helsinki accords. Among the eleven people who signed the document were Yelena Bonner, Alexander Ginzburg, Yuri Orlov and Anatoli Shcharansky. After the foundation of the Moscow Helsinki Watch Group similar groups were formed by activists in the Republics. In December 1976 the Christian Committee for the Defence of Believers' Rights was created in Moscow. Its purpose was to defend the rights of believers of any faith. It worked closely with the Moscow Helsinki Group, using the latter's channels. The committee established ties with other religious movements and engaged in some common activities. Later, human rights groups were formed by Adventists in 1978 and Pentecostals in 1980. They all based their activities on the humanitarian provisions of the Helsinki Final Act and the demand that signatory countries of the Helsinki accords observe those provisions.

All this activity put the Soviet Government in a difficult position. Three days after the formation of the Moscow Helsinki Group Orlov was warned that if he became active he and those associated with him would feel "the full force of the law".[8] Yet at the same time the Government knew that to persecute such a group would in itself constitute a violation of the Helsinki accords, and no moves were made until February 1977 when Orlov and Ginzburg were arrested. In March Shcharansky was arrested; more arrests were carried out between 1977 and 1979; and in 1980 Sakharov was exiled to the closed city of Gorki. Sadly, the Helsinki groups have not yet achieved their goal of moderating the repressive measures of the Soviet Government with the help of Western mediation. Some people will argue that President Carter should have adopted a more aggressive stance with the Soviets. As it was the Soviet Government lost a great deal of prestige abroad, but it was prepared to sacrifice this in order to retain control of its own citizens. Today the Helsinki groups are in tatters, but they have served to inform opinion both inside the USSR and abroad. By the late 1970s a formidable number of documents had been collated, bearing witness to the plight of believers and other prisoners of conscience in the USSR.

More recently, on 5 November 1984, following three days of discussion by the Human Rights Committee of the UN in Geneva, the current Soviet delegation was presented with a range of questions raised by the Western members of the Committee. The following points were made:

1. The need for official approval of all religious activities in the USSR, except religious services in a properly registered building.
2. The right of the media to propagate anti-religious

propaganda, while the religious communities have no right of reply.

3. The registration of religious communities contradicts the USSR Constitution under the principle of separation of Church and State.
4. Particular difficulties of the Roman Catholic Church in Lithuania such as the lack of publications and Bibles as well as problems at Kaunas Seminary.
5. The possibility of the Pope visiting Catholics in the Soviet Union.

The only reply given by the Soviet representatives reported in the Lutheran World Information report read: "Religious communities in the USSR are permitted to produce literature in considerable quantities. For example, 75,000 copies of the Bible were produced in 1983".[9]

Eleven years on from the original signing of the Helsinki Final Act in 1975 the question can be asked, What has been achieved in the field of human rights, especially religious rights, for people living under oppressive regimes? Did the Helsinki accords improve the condition of believers and other citizens of the Soviet Union, or did they merely raise people's hopes without cause and perhaps even make their plight worse? When the delegates met in Ottawa from 9 May to 17 June 1985 it was their task to examine compliance with the terms of the Helsinki Final Act on the part of signatory countries. Given the increase in tension between East and West and the differing definitions or emphases on what constitutes a basic and important human right in socialist regimes and Western ones, the cross-fire of accusations and examples of alleged violations was not surprising. The failure to agree a final document was not surprising either.

How then does one evaluate the Ottawa meeting, and the whole Helsinki process? There is little evidence to show that the religious rights of believers are better protected now than they were before 1975. In fact the new legislation introduced in the USSR since 1983 has even further restricted individuals' rights and hopes for justice under the law. We must also remember the invasion of Afghanistan, the Korean airliner shot down over the USSR, the imprisonment of the founder of the Christian Committee for the Defence of Believers' Rights in the USSR, and the crushing of Solidarity in Poland. Many of those in Eastern European countries who organised monitoring groups to report on their countries' observance of the terms of the Helsinki Final Act have been systematically imprisoned or forced to emigrate. The number of known Christian prisoners in the Soviet Union rose to almost 400 in 1982, and at present stands at about 320. (The total number of religious prisoners both Christian and non-Christian is approximately 400). The harsh treatment of the Jews in the USSR and sharp decrease in the number of exit visas being given to both Jews and Pentecostals has been well documented.[10] Thus the record of human rights violations in the USSR since 1975 does little to prove that they have upheld the terms of signed international agreements.[11]

There is, perhaps, a final consolation. Helsinki was, at least, the beginning of a process. As US Ambassador Richard Shifter, a delegate at Ottawa, said: "We must keep in mind that a meeting such as Ottawa was unthinkable as recently as fifteen years ago. The notion that governments might monitor the behaviour of other governments towards their own citizens, that there would be international conferences at which the domestic practices of the participating countries would be subjected to scrutiny is one of very recent origin. While the results might be meagre in their initial stage, they might be more plentiful in the future. What this means is that we ought to give the CSCE (Conference on Security and Cooperation in Europe) process further time to evolve before passing judgement on whether it has accomplished anything and whether the results justify our investment of effort".[12]

# 9

# The Secret Report to the Central Committee

Throughout this book we have cited paragraphs from the law and snippets from the Soviet press to establish what the regime's official policy towards believers is. No detailed coherent statement of this policy exists.

In 1980, however, a document was smuggled to the West which perhaps provides us with the next best thing. It appears to be a report on the state of the Russian Orthodox Church in the USSR by the Council for Religious Affairs (CRA) for the eyes of top Party members only. The copy is a numbered one and signed by V. Furov, a Vice-Chairman of the CRA. It has been carefully analysed in the West and is thought to be authentic, although with documents of this kind there is always the possibility of KGB disinformation.

Despite the absolute separation of Church and State laid down by the Constitution, this report speaks quite bluntly of the control which the authorities are seeking to exercise over the Orthodox Church. CRA representatives have regular conversations with bishops and priests, monitor all their words and activities, and write reports on them. No bishop is consecrated or transferred without a painstaking check of the candidate by the CRA in close cooperation with the KGB. The report claims that the CRA is working in the best interests of the Soviet State, and says it is interested chiefly in the political implications of the activities of churchmen. In practice this means that the CRA tries to discourage any activity by churchmen, even activity of a purely religious nature.

The writer of the document obviously wants to present the CRA in a favourable light to members of the Central Committee. Nevertheless, the tone of the report is factual, and the assessment both of the nature and effectiveness of the work of the CRA with believers, and of the difficulties still to be overcome, seem to be realistic. The writer makes no reference to the Soviet Constitution or to the laws on religion, except to point out how the clergy infringe them. There is no discussion on what the CRA is allowed to do in law, but only what it is in fact doing in order to promote the interests of the authorities. The assumption that the law is irrelevant gives the report a ring of bureaucratic cynicism which makes one feel it is genuine.

The first section of the report deals with the hierarchs of the Orthodox Church. It points out that the episcopate is the most important office in the Russian Orthodox Church, "without whose authorisation the priests and deacons do nothing". "In his diocese the bishop is the autonomous leader, whose role is to affirm and propagate the Orthodox faith and piety of his flock, eliminate errors and superstitions . . . to ordain and appoint priests and other members of the clergy, supervise their conduct and direct their activity in all domains".[1] Yet, the report continues, while today the episcopate still has great power in the Church, nonetheless, under the Soviet system it has lost many of its privileges and its limits are closely defined by the legislation on religious cults.

The author divides the bishops into three categories. First there are those whom he considers patriotic and totally loyal to the Soviet State, who respect and carry out the legislation on religious cults, and who encourage their clergy to do the same. These would include those who "are aware that our state does not wish to see an increase in the role played by religion and the church in society, and who do not display any particular zeal in spreading the influence of Orthodoxy among the population". This group contains the names of seventeen bishops including Patriarch Pimen.

Six have since died, one has retired, and the rest still retain their appointments. The second group consists of those who are loyal to the State and carry out the letter of the law on cults, but who appoint and encourage "enthusiastic" priests. There are twenty-three bishops in this category. Four have now died, and four have changed diocese. The third group are bishops who "still attempt to evade the legislation on religious cults". Of the seventeen in this group, only six are still occupying the same diocese, and five have been transferred.[2]

We can conclude from this that the Soviet authorities are interested to know the political position of bishops vis-a-vis the Soviet State, how they react to its internal and external policies, and laws on cults, and to discover the extent of their religious zeal. Thus the CRA and its local representatives will devote a great deal of time to the discussions of the Synod, as well as to the individual activities of bishops themselves. Indeed, as we have already pointed out, no bishop will be consecrated without first being closely scrutinised by the CRA. Of course those bishops chosen to work abroad will have an even greater responsibility for they will be the representatives of the State as well as caring for the interests of the Orthodox Church.

The CRA will be very careful to inform the Patriarch of the precise qualities required in a bishop, and although the Patriarch will put forward names they will have to be approved by the Council. Thus the bishop's function is moulded politically as well as ecclesiastically. For example, when handing the episcopal cross to the newly consecrated Bishop Viktorin of Perm and Solikamsk in June 1973, Patriarch Pimen said: "Bring up the children of the Church in the love of the Holy Orthodox Church and our beloved Fatherland, remembering constantly the words of Metropolitan Filaret of Moscow, according to which a bad citizen of the earthly kingdom is equally without worth in a heavenly kingdom".[3] And in reply Metropolitan Viktorin said that he would take on the responsibility "by educating the flock entrusted to him in the love of our dear

Fatherland".[4] This sort of talk is the result of a vast and systematic educational operation carried out amongst the clergy at all levels, which encourages them to become responsible members of the Soviet State. The State has elaborated a system of political education of bishops and clergy in order to develop their patriotism. Moreover, as we have mentioned before, the Church will be asked to give large sums of money to the Peace Fund, which was formed in 1961 to provide financial aid to people struggling "against Imperialism, for independence and social progress".[5]

The Soviet authorities want bishops who will comply with them and who will remain as inactive as possible in matters of religion. These, they claim, hold a "realistic" view of the situation and understand the policy of the State. The report goes on to quote the Council delegate for the territory of Stavropol, Comrade Narizhny, who provides a good example of what the authorities want in a bishop:

> There has been no important change in the activity, spiritual disposition and behaviour of Bishop Iona. As before, although he celebrates regularly, he shows no particular zeal in the pontifical offices. He regularly preaches sermons, but they are brief, with little expression and without fervour. He almost always finishes with an appeal to live in peace, to fight for peace throughout the world, to donate money to the Peace Fund and to work hard.
>
> During the seven years that he has been head of the diocese, he has not entered a single country church in the territory. He is often ill and takes himself off to the Moscow area "to rest and exhibit himself to doctors", as he says. He is not very active in his contacts with the Patriarchate: "I do not like, he says, to bother the bosses", but he reports on his affairs more often than in the past.[6]

Of course, such an amazing portrait of a bishop is capable of several interpretations. It does at least show, however, what the informant thinks his superiors want to hear.

It is evident from the Furov Report that the authorities are worried by dynamic bishops. For example in the Vladimir region Archbishop Nikolai is reported to be trying to strengthen and rejuvenate the church and without infringing the law has taken the following measures to encourage the faithful:

> he has increased the number of Pontifical services, which take place with solemnity, generally with a large crowd of people;
> he expects of the clergy "to preach more often, and not to be idle" and, in fact, the number of sermons has increased;
> he has supplied the members of the clergy and the religious organisations with a sufficient quantity of cult objects;
> he supplies the parish with personnel in good time, which has prevented the interruption of worship in the churches through lack of priests.

Bishop Nikolai had already been transferred to Vladimir by the authorities in Rostov-on-Don region where he has a reputation for religious dynamism. Since then he has been transferred again, first to the see of Kaluga in 1975, and then to Gorki in 1977.[7]

A further example is Bishop Chrysostom of Kursk, who until 1974 was Deputy Head of the Foreign Relations Department in the Patriarchate. He insists that his primary job as bishop is to find priests to fill the parishes. He says that the lack of new ordinands is extremely worrying. The seminaries are not accepting enough students, and refuse to admit any ex-members of the Komsomol. Chrysostom points out:

> My predecessor Bishop Nikolai did not receive the faithful. I receive them and I try to give them hope that their church will again have a priest. In the diocese at the moment about forty churches are closed for lack of priests. As deputy head of Department of External Relations in the Patriarchate, as a bishop, I do not want the people to complain: "This bishop is an atheist, a Chekist" as they sometimes do about us. I want to be a bishop without stain in the eyes of the faithful and foreigners. As to the delegates' accusations regarding me,

claiming that I am reviving the church, I do not tour round the churches, I do not go round inciting the faithful to take action to get churches opened. It is they themselves who come to me. I am a bishop. I am 40 years old. I have no intention of leaving the church. Although I have been subjected to many insults and injuries at the hands of atheists, now is not the time to sit with arms folded.[8]

We can see why the Council are worried by Bishop Chrysostom, because he clearly wants to strengthen the Church and has succeeded in doing so.

In the Russian Orthodox Church the Bishop will delegate some of his pastoral responsibilities to a Dean. He is rather the equivalent of the Rural Dean in the Church of England, and like him will often be a parish priest himself. The report says that many Deans are dynamic and encourage the religious life. Here for example is what the CRA representative for the region of Tomsk, Comrade Dobrynin reports:

In 1974, at the instigation and under the influence of the Dean, A. I. Pivovarov, the Orthodox clergy in the region have redoubled their efforts to spread the influence of religion within the population. At the beginning of the year, during Lent, Pivovarov declared from the pulpit that the faithful could ask a priest to visit them at home, in any district and in any village. This news spread rapidly among the believers and, from every corner in the region, came letters from the faithful asking that a priest be sent to them.

The Dean and his subordinates, interpreting in their own way the right to hear confessions of those who are gravely ill and to give them extreme unction, make use of it to practise, in the flats of the faithful, collective rites on people who are apparently in good health.

Each visit of a priest to a district where there had not been one for many years caused a sensation, rekindled the religious feelings of the faithful, aroused an unhealthy interest among unbelievers and those hitherto indifferent and, in short, answered to the interests of religious propaganda. We have taken steps to put an end to this sort of thing.[9]

The report also puts the worst construction on this, and claims that many bishops and deans will visit parishes as often as possible to earn money. The CRA representative in the region of Rostov-on-Don, Comrade Politiko, writes for example:

> Ioasaf, the resident bishop, is a man of the church who is experienced and wily. He is a monk with fanatical faith and in the past was the superior of a monastery. He deploys much effort and craftiness to revive religious activity in the region. He reacts badly to the Council representatives' recommendations and hides behind all sorts of excuses to avoid carrying them out. The diocesan council has only a formal existence and is not involved with the administration of the diocese; the bishop takes care of everything on his own. He is avid for money. On his arrival in Rostov he arranged a salary of 100 roubles a month for himself; he also receives 300 roubles a month as expenses for entertaining guests; he is fed and housed in the bishop's residence, that is to say at the expense of the diocesan administration. It is known from trusted sources that after every pontifical service celebrated outside the Rostov region he receives money secretly; an envelope with 150 to 200 roubles.[10]

The report cites other instances of bishops who engage in blackmail and corruption for financial gain. However, the overall picture given is that the bishop's annual visit to the Patriarch will usually be accompanied by another interview with the CRA, who will be able to discover something of the temperature of the diocese, as well as the attitude of the bishop himself.

The Council will also take a detailed interest in the clergy, in the first instance the priests, who can celebrate and preside at the Liturgy. The diaconate has a special role in the Russian Orthodox Church, and is not merely thought of as a stage on the way to priesthood. They will, for example, read the Gospel, intone prayers, and generally contribute to the solemnity of the service. However, the Liturgy can be celebrated without them. The lectors (psalomshchiki) read parts of the service not reserved for the priest or deacon. The report recognises that the clergy as a whole preach doctrine and so can have a direct influence on believers. Because of this the CRA will hold individual interviews with the clergy to inform them of Soviet laws on religion, and generally try to steer them towards the national interest.

In its analysis of the clergy the report makes the following observations. First there is an acute shortage of clergy. On 1 January 1975 it was estimated that there were 7,062 registered churches, but only 5,994 priests. Therefore, if those churches without a priest are to be kept open some clergy will have to serve more than one parish. Second, 55% of priests have only primary education. Only 139 have had higher education. 3,464, or 67.7%, have had higher or secondary theological education. More then 40% have undergone no theological preparation at all.[11] In spite of this the Council regard the clergy as a whole as a hardened ideological adversary: "It has devoted itself for hundreds of years to the indoctrination of the faithful, it knows how to influence them, it knows how to preach". This point is driven home by the Council delegate in the Kherson region who observes that while there is a shortage of clergy, "it has not led to an obvious diminution of religious practice. The religious associations have adapted to these different conditions and are not in jeopardy. Their revenues increase from year to year. The number of rites has been augmented".[12]

The report, then, makes the following general points about the clergy. First, that studies carried out over many years confirm that the majority are loyal to the Soviet State and comply with the laws on religious cults. The Council representative in Kiev, Comrade Rudenko, writes:

Churchmen now have an easy life; they are loyal to the state, they celebrate the cult for which they receive a salary and gifts in kind, they pay taxes and collect sickness benefit for the greater part of the month when they do not work, they look after themselves and rest. However, in the short time during the week devoted to "work", they work very hard, and in a very "productive" way, and make no less from it than they did ten or fifteen years ago. There is a curious contradiction in the attitude adopted towards clergymen: on the one hand, because of their religious influence, the number must be reduced, on the other hand, the number of believers does not diminish and the need of priests increases; on the one hand they must be compromised, and on the other, they are loyal and carry on their activity within the law, they know a great deal and can be very influential; for the latter reason it is in our interest to carry out some work among them. [13]

Second the report accuses some priests of lacking moral fibre and so not carrying out their duties properly. Comrade Malesha, the Council representative in the Bryansk region reports: "A man who is vulgar by nature, swears like a trooper and caresses the bottle, the priest Proselkov (from the village of Kletnya) tries to be on good terms with the local authorities and adapts himself to the situation. One day during the service, when he was swinging the censer in the middle of the church, he caught sight of the secretary of the district executive committee. Without pausing in the service and maintaining the rhythm of the prayer, he intoned: 'I see you, Vassili Maximovich, I see you'." And according to the report there are numerous examples of priests stealing and making themselves rich at the expense of parishioners.

There is, however, a third group who do infringe the laws on religious associations, and the report says, in so doing are not loyal to the Sate. The example quoted at some length is Father Dimitri Dudko, about whom we have written in chapter 3. Another less dramatic example is the priest V. Votyakov from Kalinovka village in the Tambov region. According to the local people he demonstrates "wild fanaticism". He holds services which last five or six hours, he checks whether the faithful are wearing a cross around the neck, and if they are not he makes them go and get one immediately or he refuses them communion. He illegally forbids his daughters to join the Pioneers or to participate in social activities at school. In an interview with the headmaster, he justified his action on the grounds that he had the right to bring up his children in the spirit of the Holy Scriptures.

The report sums up its findings on the clergy by saying that the bishops are now ordaining lay activists because of the manpower shortage, and that this is not a good thing because many of these activists would like to return the Church to its pre-revolutionary status. The CRA representatives watch over events very carefully, and try to neutralise the effect of over-enthusiasm as far as possible. But finally they are worried that the clergy is producing a caste in Soviet society which is incompatible with communism.

There follows the all-important question of how priests should be selected and trained. The Council will not allow fanatics, extremists, and the mentally ill to enter theological academies,[14] and the report cites examples of those not allowed to sit the entrance examination. Patriarch Pimen summarised the aims of the authorities in a letter to the Moscow Academy and Moscow Seminary on 14 October 1974. "The future pastors of the church," he said, "should be educated in the spirit of patriotism, for it is the moral foundation of the unity of the state and the power of our earthly motherhood". On the occasion of the sixtieth anniversary of the Moscow Theological Academy in 1974 the rector Archbishop Vladimir concurred: "The church has called and still calls us to be on the side of the people, to be patriots of our motherland, for a bad citizen of the earthly motherland cannot be a good citizen of the heavenly motherland. In building up the blessed organisation of the church never forget that you are one flesh with the Russian people, which is a great nation, a nation of builders".[15]

The Council, then, want to make certain that theological students are educated in patriotism and love of country.

They will achieve this by making the right staff appointments and by keeping a close check on the syllabus. For example, the President of the Education Committee of the Moscow Patriarchate, Metropolitan Alexi, has introduced the following items into the moral theology programme:

> True patriotism and love of the motherland as a natural requirement of the soul;
> the sacred character of military duty and work in the service of the people and the state;
> strict respect for the laws of the country and ways of contributing to its prosperity;
> one of the tasks of the Orthodox pastor: to educate the faithful in a love of the motherland and Soviet patriotism, to encourage them to work honestly and conscientiously for the good of the country;
> what is the Soviet motherland? What is a Soviet citizen?[16]

The authorities hope that by such methods they will succeed in steering the clergy away from what they call "mystico-religious" ideas, and make them into useful Soviet citizens.

At the Odessa seminary, the Furov report tells us, lectures were given on the following subjects:

> The success of the Communist Party of the Soviet Union and the Soviet Government in their struggle to put into operation the peace programme outlined by the twenty-fourth Party Congress:
> V. I. Lenin and the cultural revolution;
> communist morality concerning the attitude towards work and socialist property;
> the formation of the new man, one of the essential objectives of the building of communism;
> the teaching of Lenin on communist morality and the fundamental principles of moral education;
> the unity of the party and the people, key to all the victories of the building of communism;
> the internal and foreign policy of the Communist Party of the

Soviet Union, as the expression of the vital interests of the people.[17]

The Council representative from the Odessa region, Comrade Gavrilov, advises: "A political information meeting on current affairs in the country and abroad is organised at the seminary every week. Two lectures are given each month, entitled, 'Before the map of the World' and 'Before the map of the country'. Film shows are arranged together with pro-Soviet news documentaries. It has now become customary for the seminarists to gather every evening at 9 o'clock in the lecture hall to watch the news on television".[18]

In these ways the State controls the training of priests entering the ministry of the Russian Orthodox Church. It controls and influences recruitment; takes steps to avoid religious fanatics entering religious establishments, whether to teach or study; revises text books; introduces new courses which encourage political awareness; and most important of all attempts to reduce religious zeal in the clergy.

The report then turns its attention to the *Journal of the Moscow Patriarchate* (*JMP*). As we explained in Chapter 6 this is one of the few legal religious publications, and as a result the authorities keep a close check on it. The JMP first appeared in 1931, only to disappear again in 1935. It resumed publication in September 1943. The personnel of the *Journal* consists of an editorial staff who have had some theological training, as well as technical agents. Together they publish, administer, and distribute the *Journal*. It is published in Russian and English. The publication is supervised by the CRA, who allow only 15,000 copies to be printed in Russian each month. It is estimated that there are about 6,000 to 7,000 open Orthodox churches in the Soviet Union, and as a percentage of the *JMP* is sent to libraries abroad, the number of journals reaching churches within the USSR is small. Circulation is therefore too restricted for the *Journal* to reach ordinary lay people. Besides the *Journal* the Patriarchate is allowed to publish 5,000 copies of the *Orthodox Liturgical Calendar*, which is printed in paperback. This gives details of Feast days, Saints days, and references for daily Bible readings. It is indispensable for priests, deacons and lectors, but is just as useful for lay people who want to follow the Liturgy.

The Patriarchate is allowed to print 10,000 copies of the Patriarch's Christmas and Easter messages, as well as one million burial bands and prayers of absolution for use at religious funerals. According to the tradition of the Russian Orthodox Church when a corpse is laid in the coffin a band is placed around the brow depicting Christ with the Blessed Virgin Mary and St John the Baptist. During the service the priest reads over the deceased a prayer of absolution, whose text is printed on a sheet of paper which he then places in the right hand of the dead person. The coffin remains open until the end of the funeral. In the absence of really accurate statistics on religious practices in the USSR, the circulation figures of these funeral bands and prayers provide very interesting data. Presumably they mean that about one million funerals are carried out every year in the Orthodox churches of Russia. There is every evidence that these objects run out. According to the population survey of 1974 out of a total population of 250.9 million there were 185.6 million inhabitants of the USSR belonging to national groups with an Orthodox tradition. Given that the mortality rate was 8.7%, 1.6 million deaths occurred in the population of Orthodox tradition. It follows that approximately 60% of the deceased must have been buried by the Church. Of course, most of those never regularly attended church while alive, but this nonetheless shows some strength of religious conviction in the face of persecution and intense atheistic propaganda.[19]

Any text printed in the USSR, even tickets, dockets, and administrative forms must first be presented to a body known as Glavlit, the Central Board for the Protection of State Secrets in the Press. This is under the control of

Ministers of the USSR. However, the *Journal* and other publications of the Patriarchate are censored by the CRA on behalf of Glavlit. Censorship is considered to be very important in spite of the small circulation, because the *Journal* reaches a wide and varied circle of readers, from the ordinary parish priest to foreign readers. The *Journal* is regarded as the official mouthpiece of the Russian Orthodox Church. To quote the report: "It conveys its whole policy. It is the principal platform used by the ideologists of Russian Orthodoxy to try to defend and strengthen the position of religion and the church, to conceal from its readers the latent critical phenomena which affect the Church, to present religion as a proponent of social progress and to raise its prestige in the eyes of believers, both at home and abroad".

Obviously the very existence of an organ which provides information about religion worries the authorities. It is quite clear from the report that religious convictions are tolerated only when they are unspoken. Yet the report takes comfort from the fact that few believers will ever see the *Journal of the Moscow Patriarchate*. After citing an article which the author of the report finds particularly distasteful, he writes: "It should be noted, with reference to this point, that such publications are of no real consequence since the *Journal's* small circulation hardly ever reaches the ordinary believer".[20] However, he concludes that it is necessary to increase control over the *Journal* by "strictly monitoring the manuscripts and rejecting all propaganda promoting the 'holy places', and other documents likely to stimulate religious life".[21]

In conclusion, it may be said that when faced with Soviet reality as described in this report one has the distinct impression that all values have become reversed. It is the world of Alice through the Looking Glass. The clergy who win the author's approval are those who fail to do their job. The ideal Christian from the Soviet point of view seems to be one with a "realistic" attitude to life who, whatever his

convictions, will support Soviet "reality" without reser-
vation. Any other type is termed a "religious fanatic".
It is "fanatical" to express one's faith in any way, even to
speak about the spiritual realm. In one place the author
formulates the general conclusion that the "clergy of the
Russian Orthodox Church, although loyal to Soviet power,
nevertheless still constitute a body whose ideology is incompatible with our world view".[22] Yet at the same time he
remains worried that in spite of the shortage of priests the
church remains full of life.

# 10

# What Can We Do?

The reader may be excused for thinking that the situation of believers in the Soviet Union is so hopeless that there is nothing that can be done. But this is not the case. In this chapter I want to put forward some concrete suggestions.

First, we can pray. This can be done either as individuals, or in prayer groups where the special needs of prisoners and their families can be held up before God. There are numerous instances where prisoners have said how they were sustained by the knowledge that they were remembered in prayer. Prayer unites us to the Creator and remains the most important way in which we can help. Yet we need to be able to pray intelligently, knowing something of the prisoners' conditions and home background. Here you may need help. Keston College exists to research accurate information on the plight of believers in Communist countries, and willingly sends this to anyone interested. They put out a number of publications but its list *Christian Prisoners in the USSR* gives an up-to-date account of all known prisoners. Their address is: Keston College, Heathfield Road, Keston, Kent, BR2 6BA, England.

It is difficult to pray for everyone, but perhaps you can pick out cases from the list and adopt them in prayer. Here is one suggested prayer for the persecuted:

Lord, help us to stand by those who, for their faith and loyalty to Christ, have lost the right to worship their God and to share their faith free of state interference; to earn their living and to raise children in a manner consistent with their Christian faith. Bless, encourage, and strengthen those who suffer abuse and rejection, banishment to psychiatric hospitals, prisons, and labour camps, loneliness, heartbreak, sickness and death. Help us to help them.

Prayer can be followed by action. You may ask: "is there anything practical that I can do?" Just imagine yourself being imprisoned in the Soviet Union, separated from family and friends, hundreds or even thousands of miles from home, in difficult and harsh conditions. Then one day a letter comes from abroad. You have never heard of the sender and he doesn't say very much; just that he knows of your existence and prays for you. The effect on your morale is immeasurable. Your whole spirit is uplifted, and you are renewed. This is how a believer feels when he receives a letter from someone in the West.

Let an ex-prisoner speak for himself. This is an extract from an open letter written by Viktor Davydov, whose case was discussed in chapter 7. He is a former prisoner in a Special Psychiatric Hospital (SPH) and emigrated to the West in November 1984, largely as a result of pressure from Amnesty International who adopted him. His letter emphasises the values of letters and postcards sent to psychiatric "patients" and letters of protest sent on their behalf to the hospital administration. It can equally be applied to other forms of imprisonment in the USSR. He writes:

I have spent several years in psychiatric hospitals and have been in more than one SPH. Very little is done to help prisoners although they are detained under one of the harshest systems in the Gulag. Few people actually write to the administration of psychiatric hospitals, or try to make contact with the prisoners detained in them. Yet it is direct pressure on the hospital administration that is the most effective way of protecting human rights. This can significantly improve a prisoner's conditions of confinement and expedite his release.

The Western public has a real chance of freeing any victim of psychiatric abuse within one and a half to two years of confinement in an SPH, and within six months in an Ordinary Psychiatric Hospital. Thanks to foreign support I managed to get a range of minor privileges long before my release; these included an extension of visiting hours, the right to unrestricted mail, the right to wear my own clothes, and the opportunity to read philosophy and foreign literature. This enabled me to keep my mind lucid, and because of foreign interest in my welfare I rarely experienced brutality from the ward orderlies.

So what can be done to protect the victims of medical and physical violence and to secure their speedy release?

1. Letters can be sent to the administrators of psychiatric hospitals with persistent demands for the release of prisoners and an improvement in the conditions of their confinement, i.e. that powerful and dangerous drugs should not be administered in doses harmful to the "patient".

2. People from different places should constantly and methodically write letters to the prisoners themselves, e.g. greetings on holidays and birthdays with questions about the prisoner's mood, health and activities. Not all these letters will reach the prisoner, but they will indicate to the administrators, and to the KGB, the concern and interest of foreigners. There is indisputable proof that this changes their attitude to the prisoner for the better.

3. If a prisoner has relatives and the address is known, then you should start up a correspondence with them too. They form a channel of communication between the prisoner and his defenders.

Correspondence with prisoners is fraught with difficulties, and it is particularly hard to establish two-way contact with them. For days, months and years you may get nothing back. But only through this method can you achieve results – the key to success is to be methodical and persistent. You must not be discouraged. You must carry on writing.

How do you send a letter or postcard? Although I may have persuaded you of the need to write, it is difficult to give you accurate details in a book of this sort. You will need up-to-date advice, such as that given by the organisation Aid to Russian Christians, who can be written to at PO Box 200, Bromley, Kent, BR1 1QF, England. They will send you exact instructions, and tell you how to address the envelope, as well as give examples of greetings in Russian.

You can rest assured that you will be doing something worthwhile, as is shown in a letter recently received in the West from Igor Ogurtsov, now in exile in Mikun a thousand miles from Moscow. Mikun is the headquarters of the local Gulag, and there are many convicts working there on building projects. Thus the population consists mainly of the militia and convicts. This leaves no room for normal human contact, a lot of room for provocation, and a distrustful atmosphere. Despite serious breathing problems Ogurtsov works as a stoker. His letter, however, reflects his joy and happiness in the knowledge that he is not alone in his suffering. He writes:

My respected friend, Dear Sister in our Lord!
It was very pleasant for me to receive a few warm lines from you. It is a great feeling to sense the nearness of brothers and sisters in Christ throughout the world. I never forget all true friends in my daily prayers. Accept my greetings on the feast of the Holy Trinity and my best wishes to you and those near to you.
Unfortunately, although now, after 15 years, I have formally been given the opportunity of writing to my friends in the West, I do not expect that the letters will arrive, since I do not receive replies and the advice of delivery cards are not returned to me.
May God preserve ancient, good England!
Yours brother in Christ, I. Ogurtsov

To summarise my whole argument, the Soviet Union does not recognise the Church as a person in law. In other words the Church has no legal position in Soviet society. In the

January 1986 edition of the *Journal of the Moscow Patriarchate* it was suggested that certain revisions in the status of religious communities in the Soviet Union had either already taken place, or were in the process of taking place. However, since then there has been no concrete evidence of anything happening in practice. Thus, as things stand today any church can be closed down at any moment at the whim of the Government. For this reason successive Patriarchs have fought to keep the visible face of the Church in being. The cost at times has been awesome, not least in terms of the number of hierarchs who are now unwilling to stand up to the Soviet authorities and display indifference towards the suffering of believers who are imprisoned for their faith. However, while the Soviet Government may at this moment be unwilling to alter its policy towards believers, it is sensitive to world opinion. It claims in defence that no believer is imprisoned for his faith, but because he has violated Soviet law in some other respect. It adds that there is freedom to express religious opinion in the USSR. But much of the evidence presented in this book indicates that this is untrue.

Most important, however, is the fact that in the USSR the Church is constitutionally separated from the State and freedom of religion is guaranteed by the Soviet Constitution. Therefore, the authorities are acting illegally by interfering in the internal affairs of the Church. Indeed we can go further. The Soviet Union has also signed and ratified various international agreements which guarantee a regard for human rights. These are widely flouted, not least through the intolerable restraints placed upon the Church and believers in general, which make it all but impossible for them to lead a normal church life.

This book has sought to emphasise these issues. At first sight these problems may seem too difficult for any single individual to grapple with. It has to be admitted, moreover, that international political pressures have brought only limited success. There is not much evidence that politicians have been able to improve the lot of the average believer in the Soviet Union and any political prisoners released to the West from the USSR have usually been a part of a prisoner exchange. If the Soviet Union wants to be trusted on the international scene, it will need to be persuaded to keep its own laws and signed agreements.

Has the individual a role to play in this? I believe he has. In the first instance he can become informed, and follow this up by carrying out the suggestions made earlier in this chapter. Finally, he should be unafraid to remind politicians of public concern over these issues. The great temptation is to do nothing. This will serve to support oppression by default.

# Glossary

**AS** *Arkhiv samizdat.* Samizdat Archive, Radio Liberty, Dettinger Strasse 67, Munich.

**Bolshevik** When the All-Russian Social Democratic Labour Party (RSDRP), founded in 1898, split in 1903, those in the majority became known as Bolsheviks; in October 1917 the Bolshevik or Communist Party seized power.

**Cadre** The most important members of an organisation, those who include its nuclei of leaders at various levels.

**CCE** *Chronicle of Current Events.*

**Cheka** All-Russian Extraordinary Commission to Fight Counter Revolution, Sabotage and Speculation; established December 1917; renamed GPU in 1922; now KGB.

**Collectivisation** Establishment of Kolkhozes and Sovkhozes, which meant the end of private farming. Collectivisation began in 1917 but had made little impact by 1929 when it really got under way; was completed by 1937. Peasant opposition was dealt with brutally.

**Commissar** a) government minister; b) official representing Party, Government or Soviet.

**CPSU** Communist Party of the Soviet Union.

**CPR Bulletin** *Council of Prisoner's Relatives.* Formed in the 1960s and largely run by the wives of Baptist prisoners.

**CRA** Council for Religious Affairs.

**CSCE** Conference on Security and Cooperation in Europe.

**DCCDBR** *Documents of the Christian Committee for the Defence of Believer's Rights in the USSR.*

**Holy Synod** The committee of Bishops which advised the Tsar on the affairs of the Russian Orthodox Church. Its Chairman, the Procurator of the Holy Synod, was not a priest but one of the Tsar's most important ministers.

**JMP** *Journal of the Moscow Patriarchate.*

**KGB** Abbreviation of *Komitet gosudarstvennoi bezopasnosti* (Committee of State Security).

**KNS** *Keston News Service.*

**Kolkhoz** Collective farm; members farm land as a cooperative but in reality have little say in what is produced; this is laid down in the annual State plan. Between 1929 and 1966 there was no guaranteed basic wage, wages were paid according to the profitability of the farm. The private plot kept the Kolkhoznik and his family alive.

**Komsomol** An organisation for young people between the ages of 14 and 28. It states specifically that members must fight against religious prejudices.

**Kulak** Peasants were divided into poor, middle and rich by the Bolsheviks; the poor peasant did not have enough land to live off, the middle peasant did, and the rich peasant had enough to produce a surplus; in our terms the Kulak was a well-off farmer.

**Menshevik** When the All-Russian Social Democratic Labour Party (RSDRP), split in 1903 those in the minority became known as Mensheviks; in October 1917 the Mensheviks opposed the Bolshevik seizure of power since they believed that Russia was not ready for socialism.

**NEP** New Economic Policy. Introduced by Lenin in 1921 to alleviate the heavy burden on the population that was imposed by the Civil War (1918–1921). It permitted private enterprise and was expected to last many years, but was terminated by Stalin at the end of the 1920s and replaced by Collectivisation and the Five Year Plans.

**NKVD** People's Commissariat of Internal Affairs, renamed MVD (Ministry of Internal Affairs) in April 1946; now named KGB.

**Orthodox Church** The Russian Orthodox Church had split away from the Greek or Byzantine Orthodox Church in the sixteenth century. Thus it practised a different form of worship from the Latin or Roman Catholic Church. It was the Orthodox Church which had brought the cyrillic alphabet to Russia.

**Pioneers** Communist organisation for school children.

**Politburo** The political bureau of the Central Committee of the CPSU. The top decision-making body in the Soviet political system. It was called the Presidium between 1952 and 1966.

**Pravda** The newspaper organ of the Central Committee of the CPSU.

**RCL** *Religion in Communist Lands.*

**RSFSR** Russian Soviet Federated Socialist Republic. The official name of Soviet Russia from 1917–1922, when the USSR was formed; now the name of the largest republic in the Soviet Union, the Russian Republic.

**Samizdat** Works of literature, politics, etc. reproduced by copying, photocopying, or typing, and distributed by individuals outside the official censorship system.

**Soviet** Literally "council" – the basic government unit of the Soviet system. Also used adjectivally of the Union of Soviet Socialist Republics.

**Sovkhoz** State farm with a guaranteed minimum wage. It is run like a factory and operatives are classified as workers and as such enjoy social benefits.

**Supreme Soviet** Soviet parliament consists of two chambers, one based on nationalities, the other on demographic electoral constituencies. Only one candidate – usually proposed by the local party organisation – stands for each seat.

**Tsar** Sometimes Czar. The Emperor of Russia. An Empress ruling in her own right is a Tsaritsa. The wife of a Tsar is a Tsarina.

**Union Republics** The Soviet Union is made up of fifteen republics which are called Union republics.

**USSR** Union of Soviet Socialist Republics.

**Ukaz** A decree. The equivalent of a government order, as opposed to a legislative act.

**WCC** World Council of Churches.

**War communism** The economic order in existence between June 1918 and March 1921, when it was replaced by NEP.

# Appendix

**1917**

| | |
|---|---|
| Feb | February revolution; formation of Petrograd Soviet |
| Mar | Abdication of Nicholas II; formation of Provisional Government |
| Apr | Lenin's return to Russia |
| June | 1st All-Russian Congress of Soviets |
| | Kerensky's offensive |
| July | July days in Petrograd |
| Aug | Kornilov coup |
| Oct | October revolution; 2nd All-Russian Congress of Soviets Decrees on peace, land |
| Nov | Declaration on the Rights of the Peoples of Russia |
| | Decree on workers' control |
| Dec | Armistice on German front |
| | Creation of Cheka |
| | Finland proclaims independence |

**1918**

| | |
|---|---|
| Jan | Constituent Assembly |
| | Creation of Red Army |
| | Legislation on "separation of church and state"; Patriarch Tikhon anathematises the Bolshevik regime |
| Feb | (1st/14th) Introduction of Gregorian calendar |
| Mar | Treaty of Brest-Litovsk |
| July | Civil War (1918–21) |
| Aug | Whites capture Kazan |
| Sept | Red Terror declared |
| | German withdrawal from occupied Russian territory |

**1919**

March            Creation of Politburo

**1920**

Apr              Poland invades the Ukraine
Aug              Red Army fails to take Warsaw
Oct              Polish-Soviet armistice
Nov              Red Army defeats Wrangel in Crimea

**1921**

Feb              Creation of Gosplan
                 Red Army invades Georgia
                 Workers' unrest in Petrograd
Mar              Kronstadt revolt
                 Birth of NEP
                 Treaty of Riga with Poland

**1921–2**

                 Famine on the Volga; Government demands surrender of church valuables for famine relief
                 Civil War ends

**1922**

Feb              Cheka reorganised as GPU
Mar-Apr          11th Party Congress; Stalin becomes General Secretary
Apr              House arrest of Patriarch Tikhon
June-July        Trial and execution of Metropolitan Veniamin
Dec              Formation of Union of Soviet Socialist Republics

**1923**

Apr              First sobor of Living Church
July             USSR Constitution published

**1924**

Jan              Death of Lenin

**1925**

| | |
|---|---|
| Jan | Trotsky dismissed as war commissar |
| Apr | 14th Party Conference; "socialism in one country" accepted |

**1926**

| | |
|---|---|
| Oct | Trotsky expelled from Politburo |

**1927**

| | |
|---|---|
| May | Rupture of diplomatic relations with Britain; war scare |
| Dec | 15th Party Congress; collectivisation of agriculture resolved |

**1928**

| | |
|---|---|
| Spring | Grain procurement crisis |
| Oct | Beginning of 1st Five Year Plan (to Dec. 1932) |

**1929**

| | |
|---|---|
| Apr | Law on "religious associations" |
| Autumn | Start of forced mass collectivisation and dekulakisation |
| Nov | Bukharin expelled from Politburo; defeat of Right Opposition |

**1931**

| | |
|---|---|
| Mar | Trial of Mensheviks |

**1932**

| | |
|---|---|
| Dec | Introduction of internal passport |

**1932–4**

Famine in Ukraine and elsewhere

**1933–7**

2nd Five Year Plan

| | |
|---|---|
| **1934** | July – GPU reorganised as NKVD |
| **1935** | |
| Feb | Model collective farm statute |
| Aug | Introduction of "Stakhanovite" labour |
| Sept | Reintroduction of ranks in Red Army |
| **1936** | |
| June | Death of Gorki |
| Aug | Trial of Zinoviev, Kamenev and others |
| Sept | Yezhov succeeds Yagoda as head of NKVD |
| Dec | Promulgation of "Stalin Constitution" |
| **1937** | |
| Jan | Trial of Radek, Pyatakov and others |
| Feb | Death of Ordjonikidze |
| May-June | Dismissal, arrest, trial and execution of Tukhachevsky |
| | Powers of Red Army political commissars restored |
| **1938–**<br>**June 1941** | 3rd Five Year Plan |
| **1938** | |
| Mar | Trial of Bukharin, Rykov, Krestinsky, Rakovsky, Yagoda and others |
| Dec | Beria succeeds Yezhov as head of NKVD |
| **1939** | |
| Aug | Nazi-Soviet Pact |
| Sept | Invasion of Eastern Poland |
| Nov | Outbreak of Finnish War |
| **1940** | |
| Mar | Peace concluded with Finland |
| June | Annexation of Baltic states |
| Aug | Assassination of Trotsky in Mexico |

**1941**

| | |
|---|---|
| 22 June | German invasion of USSR |
| 3 July | Stalin's first broadcast |
| Sept | Beginning of Leningrad blockade |
| | Fall of Kiev |
| Oct | Moscow in direct danger; partial evacuation of the city |
| Dec | Wehrmacht thrown back from Moscow |

**1942**

| | |
|---|---|
| Sept | Wehrmacht reaches Stalingrad |
| Oct | Restoration of officers' full status in Red Army |
| Nov | Soviet offensive encircles German 6th Army in Stalingrad |

**1943**

| | |
|---|---|
| Jan | Surrender of German 6th Army in Stalingrad |
| July | Battle of Kursk |
| Sept | Re-establishment of Patriarchate |

**1944**

| | |
|---|---|
| Jan | Leningrad blockade finally lifted |
| June | "Second front" established in France |
| Aug-Oct | Warsaw rising |

**1945**

| | |
|---|---|
| Feb | Yalta conference |
| | Election of Patriarch Alexi |
| 9 May | Surrender of Germany |
| July-Aug | Potsdam conference |

**1946–7**

| | |
|---|---|
| | Famine in the Ukraine |

**1948**

| | |
|---|---|
| Feb | Communist coup in Czechoslovakia |
| June | Yugoslavia expelled from Cominform |

**1953**

| | |
|---|---|
| Jan | Discovery of "doctors' plot" announced |
| Mar | Death of Stalin; Malenkov becomes Prime Minister |
| May | Revolt in Norilsk labour camp |
| July | Arrest (and execution?) of Beria; revolt in Vorkuta labour camp |
| Sept | Khrushchev confirmed as first secretary of CPSU |

**1954**

| | |
|---|---|
| | Pospelov Commission begins investigation of Stalin's repressions |
| May | Revolt in Kengir labour camp |

**1954–6**

Height of "virgin lands" campaign

**1955**

| | |
|---|---|
| Feb | Bulganin replaces Malenkov as Prime Minister |
| May | Establishment of Warsaw Pact |

**1956**

| | |
|---|---|
| Feb | 20th Party Congress; Khrushchev's "secret speech" |
| Oct | Gomulka becomes first secretary of Polish United Workers' Party |
| | General strike and street demonstrations in Budapest |
| Nov | Soviet intervention in Hungary; Kadar becomes first secretary of Hungarian Workers' Party |

**1957**

| | |
|---|---|
| June | Central Committee plenum backs Khrushchev against "anti-party group" |

**1958**

| | |
|---|---|
| Feb | Khrushchev replaces Bulganin as Prime Minister |
| Oct | Pasternak awarded Nobel Prize for literature |
| Dec | Publication of new criminal code |
| | Education reforms promulgated |

**1959**

Khrushchev launches anti-religious campaign (1959–1964)

**1960**

May            Death of Pasternak

**1961**

Closure of Monastery of the Caves, Kiev
Apr            First manned Soviet space flight
First arrests at Mayakovsky Square unofficial poetry readings
July           Legislation restricting role of priest in parish councils
Oct            Stalin removed from mausoleum

**1962**

Oct            Cuban missile crisis
Nov            Publication of Solzhenitsyn's "A Day in the Life of Ivan Denisovich"

**1963**

Mar            Khrushchev addresses Writers' Union, warning of "bourgeois influences"
Autumn         Very poor harvest

**1964**

Oct            Brezhnev replaces Khrushchev as first secretary of CPSU

**1965**

Dec            Demonstration on Pushkin Square calling for observance of Soviet Constitution
Eshliman and Yakunin criticise Council for Affairs of Church in letter to Supreme Soviet

**1966**

Feb Trial of Sinyavsky and Daniel
Mar Demonstration by Baptist Initsiativniki at Supreme Soviet building in Moscow

**1967**

May Andropov succeeds Semichastny as head of KGB

**1968**

Jan Trial of Ginsburg and Galanskov
  Dubcek becomes first secretary of Czechoslovak Communist Party
Apr First issue of "Chronicle of Current Events'
Aug Warsaw Pact invasion of Czechoslovakia

**1969**

Jan Formation of Initiative Group for Defence of Civil Rights

**1972**

  First issue of "Chronicle of Lithuanian Catholic Church"
Jan Widespread arrests and searches among Ukrainian intellectuals
  Shcherbitsky replaces Shelest as first secretary of Ukrainian GP
Sept Shevardnadze replaces Mzhavanadze as first secretary of Georgian CP

**1973** Andropov and Gromyko join Politburo

**1974**

Feb Deportation of Solzhenitsyn from USSR

**1975**

Aug Helsinki agreement on European Security and Cooperation
Oct Sakharov awarded Nobel Prize for peace

**1976**          Formation of Helsinki Watch Groups in various republics

**1977**

June          Brezhnev replaces Podgorny as president of USSR
Nov          New Soviet Constitution published

**1978**

July          Trial of Shcharansky

**1979**

Apr          Brezhnev awarded Lenin Prize for literature
Dec          Soviet military intervention in Afghanistan

**1980**

Jan          Sakharov exiled to Gorki
July-Aug          Olympic Games held in Moscow
Aug          Workers' unrest in Gdansk and elsewhere in Poland; formation of Solidarity
Dec          Death of Kosygin; Tikhonov becomes Prime Minister

**1981**

Dec          Jaruzelski declares martial law in Poland

**1982**

Jan          Death of Suslov
May          Fedorchuk replaces Andropov as head of KGB; Andropov enters CP Secretariat
Sept          Last Helsinki Watch Group disbanded
Nov          Death of Brezhnev; Andropov becomes first secretary of CPSU

**1983**

Aug          Andropov falls seriously ill

**1984**

Feb          Death of Andropov; Chernenko becomes first
             secretary of CPSU

**1985**

Mar          Chernenko dies
             Gorbachev becomes first secretary of CPSU

# Notes

The author is not a Russian linguist, but has included Russian in the notes for the benefit of the Specialist.

## 2. The Russian Orthodox Church 1917–1943

1. Among the Rasputinite bishops were Makary, Metropolitan of Moscow, and Pitirim, Metropolitan of Petrograd. See Fr. G. Shavelsky, *Vospominaniya* [Memoirs], (Chekhov, New York, 1954), 2:136.

2. Gerhard Simon, "Church, State, and Society", in G. Katkov, et al., *Russia Enters the 20th Century* (Smith, Temple London, 1971), p. 28.

3. Struve, *Christians in Contemporary Russia*, p. 343.

4. *Vestnik Sviashchennogo Sinoda Pravoslavnoi Tserkvi* [Letter of the Holy Synod of the Orthodox Church], no. 1 (Moscow, 1926), 18.

5. Struve, pp. 34–35.

6. Reprinted in *VRSKhD, Vestnik russkogo studencheskogo khristianskogo dvizheniya*. [Herald of the Russian Student Christian Movement], no. 98/4 (1970), pp. 54–60. This is edited by N. Struve and maintains good contacts with Christians inside the USSR.

7. Struve, pp. 35–38. The original source of the figures appears to be the Renovationist Bishop Nikolai Solovei. See *Tserkovnyye vedomosti* [Church Gazette], no. 19–20 (October 1924), 15 (an organ of the Karlovci Synod issued from 1922 until the early 1930s).

8. *Episkopy ispovedniki* [Bishop Confessors], (San Francisco, 1971), pp. 68–70.

9. *Patriarkh Sergi i ego dukhovnoe nasledstvo*, [Patriarch Sergi and his Spiritual Inheritance]. Published in the Journal of the Moscow Patriarchate (1947), p. 61.

10. A letter (1962) by an unidentified bishop of the Catacomb Church, Regelson (*Tragediya russkoi tserkvi*, 1917–1945. p. 119 Paris: YMCA Press, 1977).

11. Hutten, *Iron Curtain Christians*, p. 11.

12. Story told to D. Pospielovsky by a Russian Orthodox priest who was born in Odessa in the mid-1920s into a religious family, and who

used to go to the church in question. As quoted in Pospielovsky, *The Russian Church under the Soviet Regime 1917–1982*, vol. 1, p. 175.

13. Fletcher, *A Study in Survival*, pp. 86–88.

14. Ibid., pp. 86–91.

15. The source has to remain unnamed. Story quoted by Pospielovsky, see above, p. 181.

16. Metropolitan Leonti letters, as quoted by Pospielovsky, see above, p. 191. Papers located in the archives of the Orthodox Church in America, Syosset, N.Y.

17. M. Popovsky, *Zhizn'i zhitiye Voino-Yasenetskogo, arkhiyepiskopa i Khirurga* [The Life of Voino-Yasenetsky, Archbishop and Surgeon], (YMCA Press, Paris 1979).

18. Alexeev and Stavrou, *The Great Revival*, pp. 100–101.

19. Ibid., pp. 101–103.

20. N. Shemetov, *Edinstvennaya vstrecha* [Sole Meeting], *VRSKhD*, no. 128 (1979), 247.

21. A Levitin-Krasnov, Memoirs. 4 vols, vol. 2, *Ruk tvoikh zhar* [Warmth of your Hands], (Tel Aviv, 1979), pp. 105–107.

## 3. The Russian Orthodox Church Since 1943

1. Patriarch Alexi, *Slova, rechi, poslaniya, obrashcheniya, doklady, stat'i* [Words, Speeches, Letters, Addresses, Reports, Articles], vol. 2 (Moscow, 1954), p. 173.

2. Konstantinow, *The Crown of Thorns*, p. 30.

3. *Pastyryam i veruyushchim greko-katolicheskoi tserkvi, prozhivayushchim v zapadnykh oblastyakh Ukrainy* [To the Ministers and believers in the Greco-Catholic Church, in the Western region Ukraine], in Patriarch Alexi, *Slova, Yechi* vol. 1 p. 121–123 (as above).

4. Fletcher, Nikolai, pp. 96–134: *Religion and Soviet Foreign Policy* p. 29.

5. "ROC (Russian Orthodox Church) Conference in Defence of Peace of All Churches and Religious Associations in the USSR", (1952), pp. 88–89.

6. I. Ratimirov. "Restavratsiya ili diskriminatsiya?" *Zemlya* [Earth or Land], *samizdat*, no. 1 (Moscow, 1 August 1974). *AS*, no. 1909.

7. For a full discussion see Bourdeaux, *Patriarch and Prophets*, pp. 300–302.

8. Ibid., p. 150.

9. Shafarevich, *Legislation on Religion in the USSR*, p. 48.

10. Ibid., pp. 13–26.

11. Struve, *Christians in Contemporary Russia*, pp. 311–320.

12. For a full account see Bourdeaux, *Patriarch and Prophets*, pp. 98–116.

13. Report anonymous, undated. (Spring 1985) p. 76. *RCL* vol. 13, no. 1.

14. N. P. Andrianov, et al., *Osobennosti sovremennogo religioznogo soznaniya* [Characteristics of Contemporary Religious Awareness], (Moscow, 1966), pp. 208–215.

15. V. D. Kobetsky, "Issledovaniye dinamiki religioznosti naseleniya", in *Ateizm, religiya, sovremennost'*, [Research on the dynamics of the Religious Population in Atheism, Religion, Contemporary Life], (Leningrad, 1973), pp. 170–1, as quoted in Pospielovsky, The Russian Church under the Soviet Regime 1917–1982, vol. 2, p. 357.

16. *Nauka i religiya* [Science and Religion] no. 2 (1963); translated by D. A. Lowrie in *RCDA* (Religion in Communist Dominated Areas) Pub N.Y. (20 May 1963), pp. 74–75.

17. Letter to Dr Potter, Secretary-General of the World Council of Churches, from A. Ogorodnikov, 27 July 1976. *RCL* vol. 4 no. 4 winter (1976), pp. 45–47.

18. T. Beeson, *Discretion and Valour*, pp. 87–88.

19. "Report of Father Gleb Yakunin to the Christian Committee for the Defence of Believers' Rights in the USSR on the Current Situation of the Russian Orthodox Church and the Prospects for a Religious Renaissance in Russia", 15 August 1979, published in *DCCDBR*, vol. 11; and also *Arkhiv samizdata* no. 3751.

20. *Russkaya mysl'* [Russian Thought], (27 September 1979), p. 4.

21. The full text of these amendments is in Vedomosti Verkhovnogo Soveta RSFSR [Gazette of the Supreme Soviet of the RSFSR], no. 27 (3 July 1975), pp. 487–491. For difficulty in opening churches see *RCL* 6:1 (1978) p. 45: 7:4(1979) pp. 258–61: 8:2(1980), p. 152.

22. *Russko vozrozhdeniye* [Russian Renaissance], no. 9 (1980), pp. 38–43. As quoted by Pospielovsky, *The Russian Church under the Soviet Regime 1917–1982*, vol. 2, p. 458.

23. Pospielovsky, p. 459.

## 4. A Background to Soviet Laws on Religion

1. Karl Marx, "Contribution to the Critique of Hegel's Philosophy of Law", in Karl Marx, Frederick Engels, *Collected Works*, vol. 3 (Progress, Moscow, 1975), p. 175. As quoted by A. Barmenkov in *Freedom of Conscience in the USSR* (Progress, Moscow, 1983), p. 10.

2. Ibid. p. 11.

3. V. I. Lenin, "Socialism and Religion", *Collected Works*, vol. 10 (Progress, Moscow, 1978), pp. 83–84. Barmenkov P. 12.

4. Lenin, "The Collapse of the Second International", *Collected Works*, vol. 21 (Progress, Moscow, 1974), pp. 231–32. Quoted in Barmenkov p. 12.

5. Lenin, The Attitude of the Workers' Party to Religion, *Collected Works*, vol. 15 (Progress, Moscow, 1977), p. 406. Quoted Barmenkov p. 15.

6. Lenin, Socialism and Religion, *Collected Works*, vol. 10, p. 86. Quoted in Barmenkov p. 15.

7. One dessiatine = 2.7 acres. Quoted from Lenin, "To the Rural Poor", in *Collected Works, vol. 6*, (1974), p. 376.

8. Ibid.

9. A. Barmenkov, *Freedom of Conscience in the USSR*, pp. 15–16.

10. F. Garkavenko, *On Religion and the Church, a Collection of Documents*, (Moscow, 1965), pp. 95, 119.

11. "On Separation of Church from State and School from Church", in "Collection of Laws and Decrees of the Government of Workers and Peasants of the RSFSR", no. 18 (26 January 1918); reprinted in Garkavenko, *On Religion and the Church*, p. 96.

12. A facsimile of the first text of the decree with an added handwritten note by Lenin "Tsirkulyar po voprosu ot otdelenii tserkvi ot gosudarstva", *Voprosy istorii religii i ateizma* [Problems of the history of religion and Atheism] 5 (1958), p. 34.

13. P. V. Gidulyanov, *Church and State in the Legislation of the RSFSR*, (Moscow, 1923), p. 27, as quoted in J. S. Curtiss, *The Russian Church and the Soviet State, 1917–1950*, (Boston, 1953), p. 76.

14. Gidulyanov, *The Separation of Church from State; complete collection of decrees of the RSFSR and the USSR; instructions, circulars etc. With interpretations of the fifth department of the People's Commissariat of Justice of the RSFSR*, 2nd edn, (Moscow, 1924), pp. 207–8.

15. Ibid, pp. 203–25; 369–70. See also Garkavenko "On Religion", pp. 105–9.

16. Gidulyanov, *The Separation of Church from State*, revised edition, (1926), pp. 55–56.

17. Ibid.

18. "Ordinance of the All-Russian Central Executive Committee of the Soviets and the Council of People's Commissars", *in Sobraniye uzakonenii i rasporyazhenii rabocke-krest'yanskogo pravitel'stva*, RSFSR, no. 35 (1929), text no. 353; amendments in no. 8 (1932), text no. 41 11 6.

19. "*The Law on Religious Associations of the RSFSR and laws and instructions in force, with individual commentaries*", (Moscow, 1930).

20. United Nations, Commission on Human Rights, Subcommission on the Prevention of Discrimination and the Protection of Minorities, "*Study of Discrimination in the Matter of Religious Rights and Practices*", conference room paper no. 35 (30 January, 1950). This is a summary of information relating to the USSR by special reporter Areot Krishnaswami.

21. "*Constitution of the Union of Soviet Socialist Republics*", (Moscow 1959), p. 26. Article 124 of the Constitution states: "In order to ensure to citizens

freedom of conscience, the Church in the USSR is separated from the State, and the School from the Church. Freedom of religious worship and freedom of anti-religious propaganda are recognised for citizens".

22. "Materials of the 22nd Congress of the CPSU", (Moscow, 1961), p. 412. Reprinted in *On Religion* pp. 82–83.

23. "*Legislation on Religious Cults (Collection of materials and documents)*". Published by Yuridicheskaya Literatura, Moscow (1971). Ed. V. A. Kuroyedov, Chairman CRA, and written by A. S. Pankratov, Deputy Procurator General of the USSR; 2nd edn. This says on the title page: "For Official Use Only", and is one of 21,000 numbered copies. This one was smuggled out of the Soviet Union.

24. I. R. Shafarevich, "*Legislation on Religion in the USSR*", p. 68.

25. D. A. Loeber, "Legal Rules. For Internal Use Only", *The International and Comparative Law Quarterly*, (January 1979), p. 77.

## 5. Application of the Laws

1. Extracts from the Criminal Code of the RSFSR (Russian Republic).

2. G. Yakunin, *SSSR Vnutrenniye protivorechiya* [USSR Internal Contradictions], vol. 3, p. 189.

3. *CCE* nos. 1–11 P. Reddaway (J. Cape 1972). *CCE* nos. 12–16; 17–64 (Amnesty).

4. *CCE* no. 34 pp. 137–138.

5. "List of Political Prisoners USSR", USSR News Brief, Munich. 1 May, 1982.

6. Information from Keston College.

7. Ibid.

8. W. E. Butler, *Soviet Law*, pp. 271–272.

9. Quoted from *KNS* no. 237 (31 October 1985), signed Tengiz Gudava, 30 May 1985.

10. *KNS* no. 228 (27 June 1985).

11. *KNS* no. 251 (29 May 1986).

12. For details see: *KNS* no. 242 (23 January 1986); *KNS* no. 244 (20 February 1986); *KNS* no. 247 (3 April 1986).

13. Amnesty, *Prisoners of Conscience in the USSR*, p. 44.

14. Ibid., p. 58.

15. Keston College Prisoner Profile, and *Christian Prisoners in the USSR (1985/6)*.

16. *Prisoners of Conscience in the USSR*, pp. 55–6.

17. This decree is signed by the Chairman of the Presidium of the Supreme Soviet of the USSR, Yuri Andropov, and the Secretary of the Presidium of the Supreme Soviet of the USSR, T. Mentetashvili. Information from *USSR News Brief (Vesti iz SSR)*, Munich no. 3 1984 (15 February 1984).

18. *KNS* no. 214 (6 December 1984); *KNS* no. 229 (11 July 1985).
19. *KNS* no. 226 (30 May 1985).
20. *USSR News Brief (Vesti iz SSSR)*, Munich no. 11 1984 (15 June 1984).
21. Keston internal memo (May 1985).
22. Radio Free Europe as quoted in *KNS* no. 223 Profile, (18 April 1985).
23. *RCL* vol. 13 no. 2 (Summer 1985) pp. 198–9.
24. *RCL* vol. 12 no. 2 (Summer 1984) p. 199.
25. *KNS* no. 232 (22 August 1985).

## 6. Harassment and Discrimination

1. *AS* 33 no. 2684 (1980) pp. 1–2. This figure includes adherents and children.
2. Reports of the Helsinki Accord Monitors (1979) p. 2.
3. *CCE* no. 46 p. 46.
4. Helsinki Monitors (1979) p. 77.
5. *AS* 35 no. 4423 (1981).
6. Ibid.
7. Helsinki Monitors (1979) p. 8. Again this includes adherents and children.
8. Ibid. pp. 65–68.
9. *KNS* no. 152 (1 July 1982) as quoted from *samizdat* document. The Balaks were driven to seek help at the British Embassy in Moscow 27 April 1982. Keston College understands that the family, who were detained on leaving the British Embassy, were in fact subsequently released but were still homeless.
10. *CCE*, no. 47 pp. 91–92; and no. 46 p. 52, as quoted by L. Alexeyeva, in *Soviet Dissent*, p. 238.
11. *CCE* no 46 p. 37; no 47 pp. 34–38; no 48 pp. 121–122; as quoted in *Soviet Dissent*, pp. 242–243.
12. Friedensstimme Mission (W. Germany) as reported in *KNS* no. 242 (9 January 1986).
13. *KNS* no. 227 (13 June 1985).
14. A specialist in the science of systems of control and communications in animals and machines.
15. *KNS* no. 198 (3 May 1984).
16. *Evangelical Times* (August 1984) p. 7.
17. *KNS* no. 237 (31 October 1985).
18. *KNS* no. 239 (28 November 1985).
19. *Chronicle of the Lithuanian Catholic Church*, published by Lithuanian Roman Catholic Priests, League of America, 351 Highland Blvd. Brooklyn. NY11207. (1978) No. 22.
20. From issue No. 11/1984 of the Soviet weekly *Nauka i religiya*

[Science and Religion], as quoted in *KNS* no. 217 (24 January 1985).
21. *RCL* vol. 13 no. 3 (Winter 1985) p. 315. Soviet Press Articles.
22. *RCL* vol. 12 no. 1 (Spring 1984) p. 88. Soviet Press Articles.
23. *DCCDBR* (10 October 1979). Russian original appears in *Documents of the Christian Committee for the Defense of Believers' Rights in the USSR*; vol. 12, Moscow 1979, (San Francisco; Washington Research Centre, 1980), pp. 1242–1243.
24. *CCE* no. 48 p. 124.
25. *CCE* no. 51 p. 142.
26. *Evangelical Times* (January 1985) pp. 1–2. From Friedensstimme (UK).
27. *KNS* no. 233 (5 September 1985).
28. *CPR Bulletin* 100 (11) (December 1981), pp. 12–43.
29. The Old Believers went into schism from the Russian Orthodox Church in the 17th Century.
30. Report anonymous undated one page, quoted *RCL* vol. 12 no. 1 (Spring 1984), p. 93.
31. Ibid.

## 7. Punishment

1. *CCE* (*Chronicle of Current Events*) nos. 30 and 32.
2. Amnesty, *Prisoners of Conscience in the USSR*, p. 67.
3. RFSFR "Code of Criminal Procedure", Article 201.
4. Kaminskaya, *Final Judgement. My Life as a Soviet Defence Lawyer*, pp. 346 ff.
5. Kuznetsov, *Prison Diaries*, p. 216.
6. Named after *Piotr* Stolypin 1862–1911. Pyotr Prime Minister of Russia assassinated by revolutionaries.
7. *KNS* no. 221 (21 March 1985).
8. *Prison Diaries*, pp. 20–21.
9. A Shifrin, *The First Guide Book to the USSR, to Prisons and Concentration Camps of the Soviet Union*, p. 54.
10. *Prison Diaries*, p. 22.
11. Shifrin, above, p. 62: the testimony of K. Zalman, 1975.
12. *Commentary to the RSFSR Corrective Labour Code*, (Moscow, 1973), p. 18.
13. Ibid., p. 146.
14. Ibid., p. 65.
15. V. Bukovsky, *To Build a Castle*, pp. 17–18.
16. *Chronicle of the Women's Camp in Mordovia USSR. Samizdat* document (1985).
17. Chekist. A member of the political police. The Cheka was the predecessor of the KGB (1917–1922).

18. *"Christian Prisoners in the USSR"* 1983/4 (Keston College), pp. 12–13.

19. Ibid., (1985–86), p. 12.

20. *To Build a Castle*, see above, p. 163.

21. *Information Bulletin of the International Association on Political Use of Psychiatry*. no. 1 (London May 1981), and no. 3 (March 1982).

22. Account given to the Sakharov Hearing in London March 1985.

23. *Christian Prisoners in the USSR*, (1983/4), p. 14.

24. Sakharov Hearing above.

25. *RCL* vol. 13 no. 3 p. 319, Soviet Religious *Samizdat*.


## 8. International Law

1. The Nuremberg Laws provided a legal foundation for discrimination against the Jews. Under those laws any German who could produce a baptismal certificate for all four grandparents was considered to be an Aryan, and therefore not subject to discrimination.

2. H. Lauterpacht, *International Law and Human Rights*, (London 1950); republished1968.

3. For an extended argument see Sieghart, *The International Law of Human Rights*, p. 54.

4. Sieghart, *The Lawful Rights of Mankind*, parts 2 and 3.

5. A. Amalrik, *Notes of a Revolutionary*, (New York: A. A. Knopf, 1982), p. 26.

6. *International Affairs*, vol. 61. no. 4 (Butterworth Scientific Ltd Autumn 1985).

7. "Schultz calls for renewed East–West dialogue", (17 January 1984). Address in Stockholm. (*US Information Service*, 18 January 1984).

8. *CCE* no. 9.

9. *KNS* no. 214 (6 December 1984).

10. *KNS* no. 178 (14 July 1983), pp. 9–11.

11. *KNS* no. 230 (25 July 1985).

12. Ibid.


## 9. The Secret Report to the Central Committee

1. Brockhaus and Efron's *Encyclopedia*, vol. 11a (1894), p. 662.

2. Furov, *"Secret Report to the Central Committee"* pp. 3–4, English translation.

3. Furov, above, p. 6; gives as his source: *JMP* no. 7 (1973), p. 7.

4. Ibid.

5. Furov, p. 7. A footnote to the report reads: "The civil authorities oblige the church to make very considerable contributions to this fund".

6. Furov, p. 7.

7. Furov, p. 11.

8. Furov, p. 12.

9. In the Orthodox Church many rites are celebrated in the homes of believers; e.g. house blessings, services for the dead, thanksgivings and occasionally baptisms. The decree of 1929 did not mention such celebrations, so after the war they were commonly practised. In 1961 the authorities tried to stop them, and in 1975 new alterations to the 1929 laws were introduced. One specified that any celebration of religious worship in the homes of believers must be subject to the special authorisation of the local authorities. This in practical terms means prohibition.

10. Furov, pp. 21–22.

11. If the clergy come from religious homes they will usually be excluded from higher education for being believers, and so will become a part of an underprivileged section of the population.

12. Furov, p. 26.

13. Furov, p. 31.

14. Ordination to the priesthood in the Russian Orthodox Church does not depend on academic attainment. Holiness of life and genuine vocation are considered more important. It is common for men to be ordained without formal theological training, and during the 1930s it was impossible for anyone to attend an academy or seminary anyway. An academy offers education at University level. In Russia there is one in Moscow (Zagorsk) and another in Leningrad. A seminary offers a four-year course, which can be followed by a further four years at an academy for the academically gifted student. There are three seminaries – Moscow, Leningrad, and Odessa.

15. Furov, pp. 48–49. The report gives as his source *JMP* no. 1 (1975), p. 18.

16. Furov, p. 49–50.

17. Furov, p. 51.

18. Ibid.

19. Furov, footnotes to p. 58.

20. Furov, p. 67.

21. Ibid.

22. Furov, p. 43.

# Bibliography

## Books and Articles

Alexeev, Wassilij. "The Russian Orthodox Church 1927–1945. Repression and Revival", *RCL* vol. 7, no. 1 Spring 1979.

Alexeev, Wassilij, and Stavrou T. G. *The Great Revival. The Russian Church under German Occupation*, (Burgess Publishing Company, Minneapolis, USA, 1976).

Amnesty International, *Prisoners of Conscience in the USSR*, (Quartermaine House Ltd, 1980).

Barmenkov, A. *Freedom of Conscience in the USSR*. (Progress Publishers, Moscow 1983).

Beeson, T. *Discretion and Valour*, (Collins/Fontana, London 1974; revised edition Collins/Fount, London, 1982).

Bloch, S. and Reddaway, Peter. *Soviet Psychiatric Abuse: The Shadow over World Psychiatry*, (Gollancz, London, 1984).

Bourdeaux, M. *Faith on Trial in Russia*, (Hodder and Stoughton, 1971).

*Patriarchs and Prophets: Persecution of the Russian Orthodox Church*, (reprinted Mowbrays, London and Oxford, 1975).

*Opium of the People*, (reprinted Mowbrays, London and Oxford, 1977).

*Religious Ferment in Russia: Protestant Opposition to Soviet Religious Policy*, (Macmillan, 1968). "The Black Quinquennium: The Russian Orthodox Church 1959–1964", *RCL* vol. 9, no. 1–2 pp. 18–27.

Bourdeaux, M. and Rowe, Michael. *May One Believe – in Russia?* (Darton Longman & Todd, London, 1980).

Bukovsky, V. *To Build a Castle: My Life as a Dissenter*, (Deutsch, London, 1978).

Butler, W. E. *Soviet Law*. Butterworth's Legal Systems of the World, (Butterworth, London 1983).

Conquest, R. *Religion in the USSR*, (The Bodley Head, London, 1968).

Dallin, A. *German Rule in Russia 1941–1945*, (MacMillan, London, 1957).

*Documents of the Christian Committee for the Defense of Believers' Rights in the USSR (DCCDBR)*. Published by Washington Research Centre. 3101 Washington St. San Francisco. California 94115. USA.

Dudko, Father Dimitri, *Our Hope*, translated into English by Paul Garrett, St Vladimir's Seminary Press, Crestwood, New York, 1977).

Ellis, J. *The Russian Orthodox Church: A Contemporary History*, (Croom Helm Ltd, Beckenham, Kent, 1986).

'USSR: The Christian Seminar'', *RCL*, vol. 8, no. 2 (Summer 1980).

"The Christian Committee for the Defence of Believers' Rights in the USSR". *RCL*, vol. 8, no. 4 (Winter 1980).

Fletcher, W. *Nikolai*, (Collier-Macmillan, London, 1968).

*The Russian Orthodox Church Underground, 1917–1970*, (Oxford University Press, 1971).

*Religion and Soviet Foreign Policy, 1945–1970*, (Oxford University Press, 1973).

*A Study in Survival*, (New York: Macmillan, 1965).

Furov, V. *Secret Report to the Central Committee on the State of the Church in the USSR. 1975.*

Hayward, M. and Fletcher, William, *Religion and the Soviet State*, (Pall Mall, 1969).

Hutten, K. *Iron Curtain Christians*, (Minneapolis, Augsburg Publishing House, 1967).

Kaminskaya, D. *Final Judgement: My Life as a Soviet Defence Lawyer.* (Harvill Press, London, 1983).

Konstantinow, The Very Rev. D. *Crown of Thorns* (Zarya, London, Ontario, 1979).

Kuznetsov, E. *Prison Diaries*, (Vallentine, Mitchell, 1975).

Levitin-Krasnov, A. "Save these Honest People", 7 May 1977; English translation in Yakunin and Regelson *Letters from Moscow*

"Religion and Soviet Youth". *RCL*, vol. 7, no. 4 Winter 1979.

Marshall, R. H. (ed.) *Aspects of Religion in the Soviet Union 1917–1967*, (University of Chicago Press, 1971) see J. Delaney, "The Origins of Anti-Religious Organisations" and J. Rothenberg, "The Legal Status of Religion in the Soviet Union".

Medevdev, R. *On Soviet Dissent*, (Columbia University Press, New York, 1985).

Meerson-Aksenov, M. "The Russian Orthodox Church 1965–1980", *RCL* vols 9 no. 3–4 Autumn 1981.

Pospielovsky, D. *The Russian Orthodox Church Under the Soviet Regime 1917–1982* (St Vladimir's Seminary Press, Crestwood, New York, 1984) vol. 1, 2.

Regelson L. *Tragediya russkoi tserkvi, 1917–1945.* (Paris: YMCA Press 1977).

Sawatsky, W. "The New Soviet Law on Religion", *RCL* vol. 4, no. 2 (Summer 1976).

"Secret Soviet Lawbook on Religion", *RCL* vol. 4, no. 4 (Winter 1976).

Scarfe, A. (ed.) *The CCDBR Documents: Christian Committee for the Defence of Believers' Rights in the USSR*, translated by Maria Belaeffa (Door of Hope Press and Society for the Study of Religion under Communism, Glendale/Orange, California, 1982).

Shafarevich, I. R. *Legislation on Religion in the USSR: A Report to the Human Rights Committee* (YMCA Press, Paris, 1973).

Shifrin, A. *The First Guidebook to the USSR, to Prisons and Concentration Camps of the Soviet Union*, (Stephanus Edition, Switzerland, 1980).

Sieghart, P. *The Lawful Rights of Mankind*, (Oxford University Press, 1985).

*The International Law of Human Rights*, (Clarendon Press, Oxford, 1984).

Simon, G. *Church, State and Opposition in the USSR*, Translated from the German by Kathleen Matchett, (C. Hurst & Co. London, 1974).

Solzhenitsyn, A. *Letter to Soviet Leaders*, (Fontana Books, London, 1974). *From Under the Rubble*, (Collins & Harvill Press, London, 1975).

*The Oak and the Calf*, (Harper & Row, New York, 1979).

Struve, N. *Christians in Contemporary Russia*, (Harvill Press, London, 1967).

Walters, P. "Vladimir Osipov: Loyal Opposition?", *RCL* vol. 5 no. 4 (Winter 1977).

"The Living Church 1922–1946", *RCL* vol. 6. no. 4 (Winter 1978).

"The Russian Orthodox Church 1945–1959", *RCL* vol. 8 no. 3 (Autumn 1979).

"The Ideas of the Christian Seminar", *RCL* vol. 9 nos. 3–4 (Summer/ Autumn 1981).

Ware, T. *The Orthodox Church*, (Penguin Books, Harmondsworth, Middlesex, 1963, revised 1964).

Yakunin, Father Gleb, and Regelson, Lev. *Letters from Moscow*, ed. J. Ellis, (H. S. Dakin & Company, San Francisco, 1978).

Zernov, N. "The 1917 Council of the Russian Orthodox Church", *RCL* vol. 6 no. 1 (Spring 1978).

## Periodicals

*AS* (Archiv Samizdata) Radio Liberty, Munich.

*Chronicle of Current Events*, Amnesty International, London (translation of *khronika tekushchikh sobytii*. Khronika Press, New York).

*Chronicle of the Lithuanian Catholic Church*, New York. ·

*Christian Prisoners in the USSR*. A Study by Keston College.

*Information Bulletin* of the Working Commission to Investigate the Use of Psychiatry for Political Purposes, London.

*Journal of the Moscow Patriarchate*, Moscow.

*Keston News Service*, Keston, Kent, England.

*Literaturnaya gazeta* (leading Soviet literary weekly), Moscow.

*Nauka i religiya* [Science and Religion] (leading Soviet atheist journal), Moscow.

*Novosti Press Agency*, Moscow.

*Novy mir* [New World) (leading Soviet literary monthly), Moscow.

*Radio Liberty Research*, Radio Liberty, Munich.

*Religion in Communist Lands* (*RCL*), Keston, Kent, England.

*Russkaya mysl* (*La pensée russe*), Paris. (A Russian weekly published in Paris since 1947).

*Veche*, a samizdat journal devoted to religion, Christian culture, Russian history and Russian Nationalism. Founded by Vladimir Osipov in 1971. Since 1981 an independent Russian almanac is published in Munich under the same name.

*Vesti iz SSSR* (USSR News Brief), Munich.

*VRSKhD, Vestnik russkogo Studencheskogo Khristianskogo Dvizheniya* [Herald of the Russian Student Christian Movement], Paris.

# Index